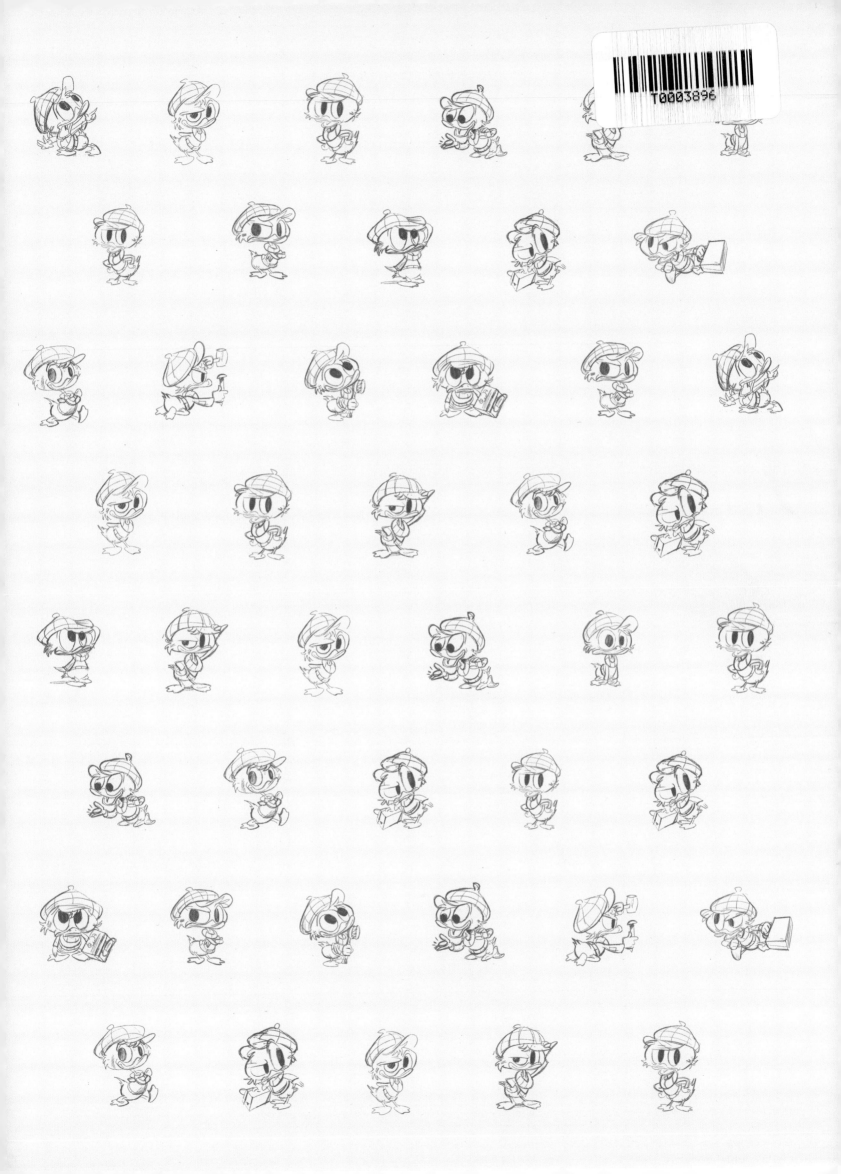

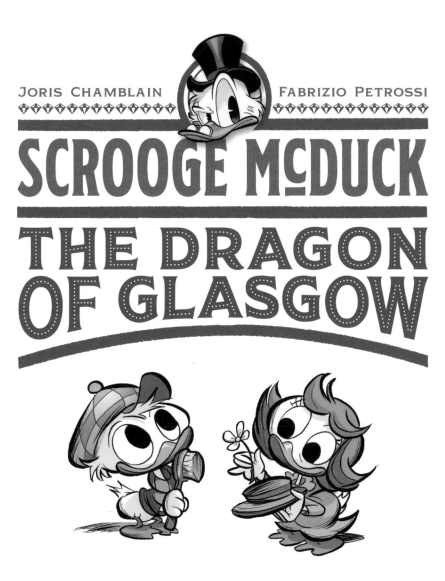

Walt Disney

JORIS CHAMBLAIN ◆◆◆◆◆◆◆◆ FABRIZIO PETROSSI

SCROOGE McDUCK

THE DRAGON OF GLASGOW

Story

Joris Chamblain

Art

Fabrizio Petrossi

Color

Bruno Tatti

with Merete Jepsen

FANTAGRAPHICS SEATTLE · WA

President/Publisher: GARY GROTH
Editor: DAVID GERSTEIN
Translator: DAVID GERSTEIN
Designer: JUSTIN ALLAN-SPENCER and ÉDITIONS GLÉNAT
Lettering and Production: PAUL BARESH and C HWANG
Associate Publisher/VP: ERIC REYNOLDS

Fantagraphics Books, Inc.
7563 Lake City Way NE
Seattle WA 98115
(800) 657-1100

Visit us at fantagraphics.com
Follow us on Twitter at @fantagraphics
and on Facebook at facebook.com/fantagraphics.

First printing: August 2023
ISBN 978-1-68396-766-8
Printed in China
Library of Congress Control Number: 2022950909

The feature story in this volume was first published in France, and appears here in English for the first time.

IN THIS SERIES

Mickey Mouse: Mickey All-Stars | 40 international artists, including Giorgio Cavazzano and Mike Peraza

Mickey Mouse: Zombie Coffee | Régis Loisel

Donald Duck: Donald's Happiest Adventures | Lewis Trondheim and Nicolas Keramidas

Scrooge McDuck: The Dragon of Glasgow | Joris Chamblain and Fabrizio Petrossi

ALSO AVAILABLE

Chip 'n Dale Rescue Rangers: The Count Roquefort Case
Bobbi JG Weiss, Doug Gray, Lee Nordling, and others; *Disney Afternoon Adventures* Vol. 3

The Complete Life and Times of Scrooge McDuck Deluxe Edition | Don Rosa

Disney One Saturday Morning Adventures | 40+ creators including Daan Jippes, Laura McCreary, and Scott Gimple

Mickey Mouse: The Monster of Sawtooth Mountain | Paul Murry; *Disney Masters* Vol. 21

TaleSpin: Flight of the Sky-Raker
Bobbi JG Weiss, Michael T. Gilbert, Romano Scarpa, and others; *Disney Afternoon Adventures* Vol. 2

Uncle Scrooge: Operation Galleon Grab | Giorgio Cavazzano; *Disney Masters* Vol. 22

Uncle Scrooge and Donald Duck in Les Miserables and War and Peace | Giovan Battista Carpi

Uncle Scrooge and Donald Duck: Bear Mountain Tales
20 American and international artists, including Carl Barks, Don Rosa, Daniel Branca, and Giorgio Cavazzano

Walt Disney's Silly Symphonies 1932-1935 Starring Bucky Bug and Donald Duck
Al Taliaferro with Earl Duvall, Merrill De Maris, and Ted Osborne

Walt Disney's Uncle Scrooge: Cave of Ali Baba | Carl Barks

Walt Disney's Uncle Scrooge: The Diamond Jubilee Collection | Carl Barks with William Van Horn and Daan Jippes

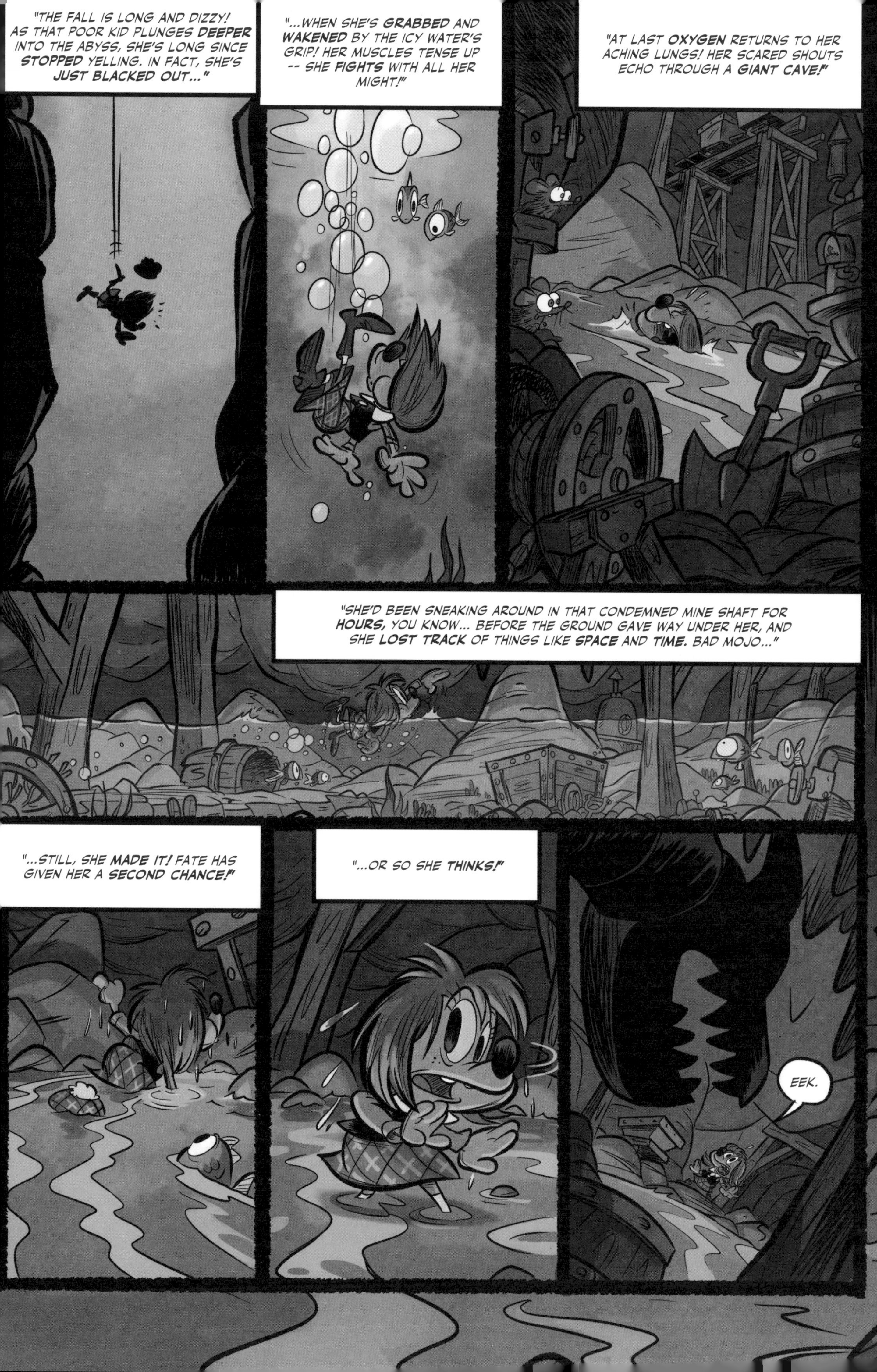
"THE FALL IS LONG AND DIZZY! AS THAT POOR KID PLUNGES DEEPER INTO THE ABYSS, SHE'S LONG SINCE STOPPED YELLING. IN FACT, SHE'S JUST BLACKED OUT..."
"...WHEN SHE'S GRABBED AND WAKENED BY THE ICY WATER'S GRIP! HER MUSCLES TENSE UP -- SHE FIGHTS WITH ALL HER MIGHT!"
"AT LAST OXYGEN RETURNS TO HER ACHING LUNGS! HER SCARED SHOUTS ECHO THROUGH A GIANT CAVE!"
"SHE'D BEEN SNEAKING AROUND IN THAT CONDEMNED MINE SHAFT FOR HOURS, YOU KNOW... BEFORE THE GROUND GAVE WAY UNDER HER, AND SHE LOST TRACK OF THINGS LIKE SPACE AND TIME. BAD MOJO..."
"...STILL, SHE MADE IT! FATE HAS GIVEN HER A SECOND CHANCE!"
"...OR SO SHE THINKS!"
EEK.

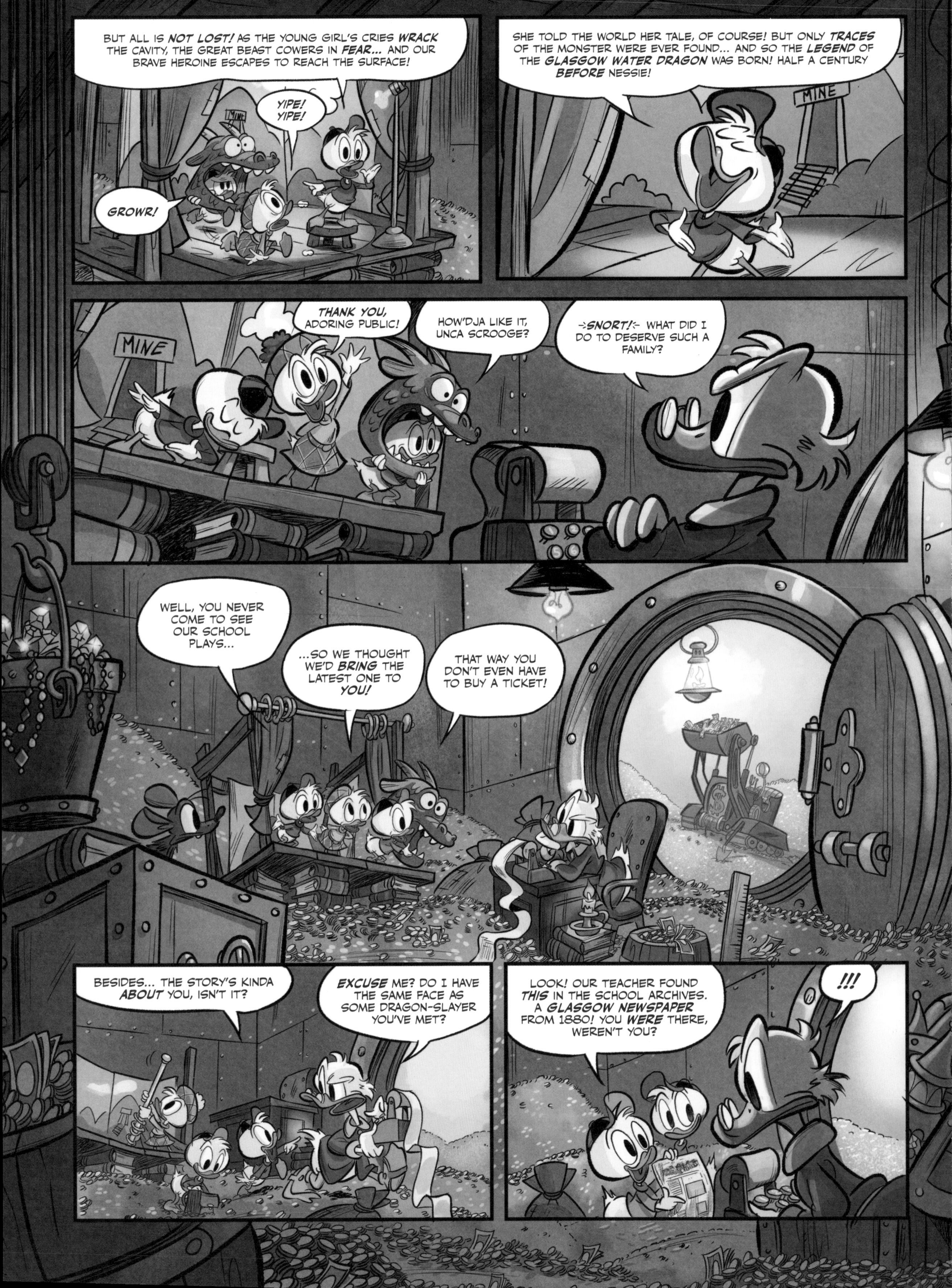
BUT ALL IS NOT LOST! AS THE YOUNG GIRL'S CRIES WRACK THE CAVITY, THE GREAT BEAST COWERS IN FEAR... AND OUR BRAVE HEROINE ESCAPES TO REACH THE SURFACE!
YIPE! YIPE!
GROWR!
SHE TOLD THE WORLD HER TALE, OF COURSE! BUT ONLY TRACES OF THE MONSTER WERE EVER FOUND... AND SO THE LEGEND OF THE GLASGOW WATER DRAGON WAS BORN! HALF A CENTURY BEFORE NESSIE!
MINE
MINE
THANK YOU, ADORING PUBLIC!
HOW'DJA LIKE IT, UNCA SCROOGE?
→SNORT!← WHAT DID I DO TO DESERVE SUCH A FAMILY?
WELL, YOU NEVER COME TO SEE OUR SCHOOL PLAYS...
...SO WE THOUGHT WE'D BRING THE LATEST ONE TO YOU!
THAT WAY YOU DON'T EVEN HAVE TO BUY A TICKET!
BESIDES... THE STORY'S KINDA ABOUT YOU, ISN'T IT?
EXCUSE ME? DO I HAVE THE SAME FACE AS SOME DRAGON-SLAYER YOU'VE MET?
LOOK! OUR TEACHER FOUND THIS IN THE SCHOOL ARCHIVES. A GLASGOW NEWSPAPER FROM 1880! YOU WERE THERE, WEREN'T YOU?
!!!

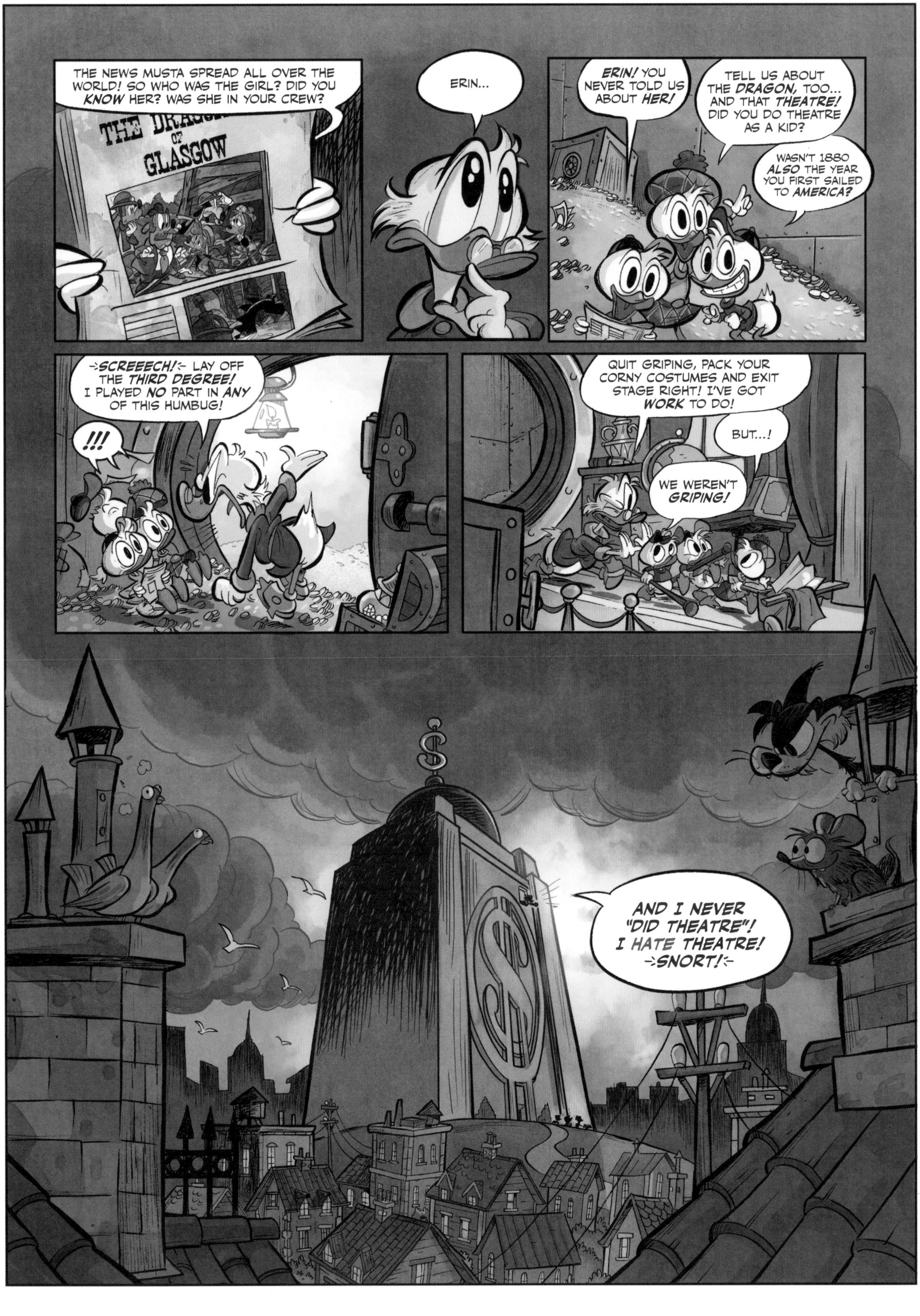

THE NEWS MUSTA SPREAD ALL OVER THE WORLD! SO WHO WAS THE GIRL? DID YOU KNOW HER? WAS SHE IN YOUR CREW?
THE DRAG... OF GLASGOW
ERIN...
ERIN! YOU NEVER TOLD US ABOUT HER!
TELL US ABOUT THE DRAGON, TOO... AND THAT THEATRE! DID YOU DO THEATRE AS A KID?
WASN'T 1880 ALSO THE YEAR YOU FIRST SAILED TO AMERICA?
-SCREEECH!- LAY OFF THE THIRD DEGREE! I PLAYED NO PART IN ANY OF THIS HUMBUG!
!!!
QUIT GRIPING, PACK YOUR CORNY COSTUMES AND EXIT STAGE RIGHT! I'VE GOT WORK TO DO!
BUT...!
WE WEREN'T GRIPING!
AND I NEVER "DID THEATRE"! I HATE THEATRE! -SNORT!-

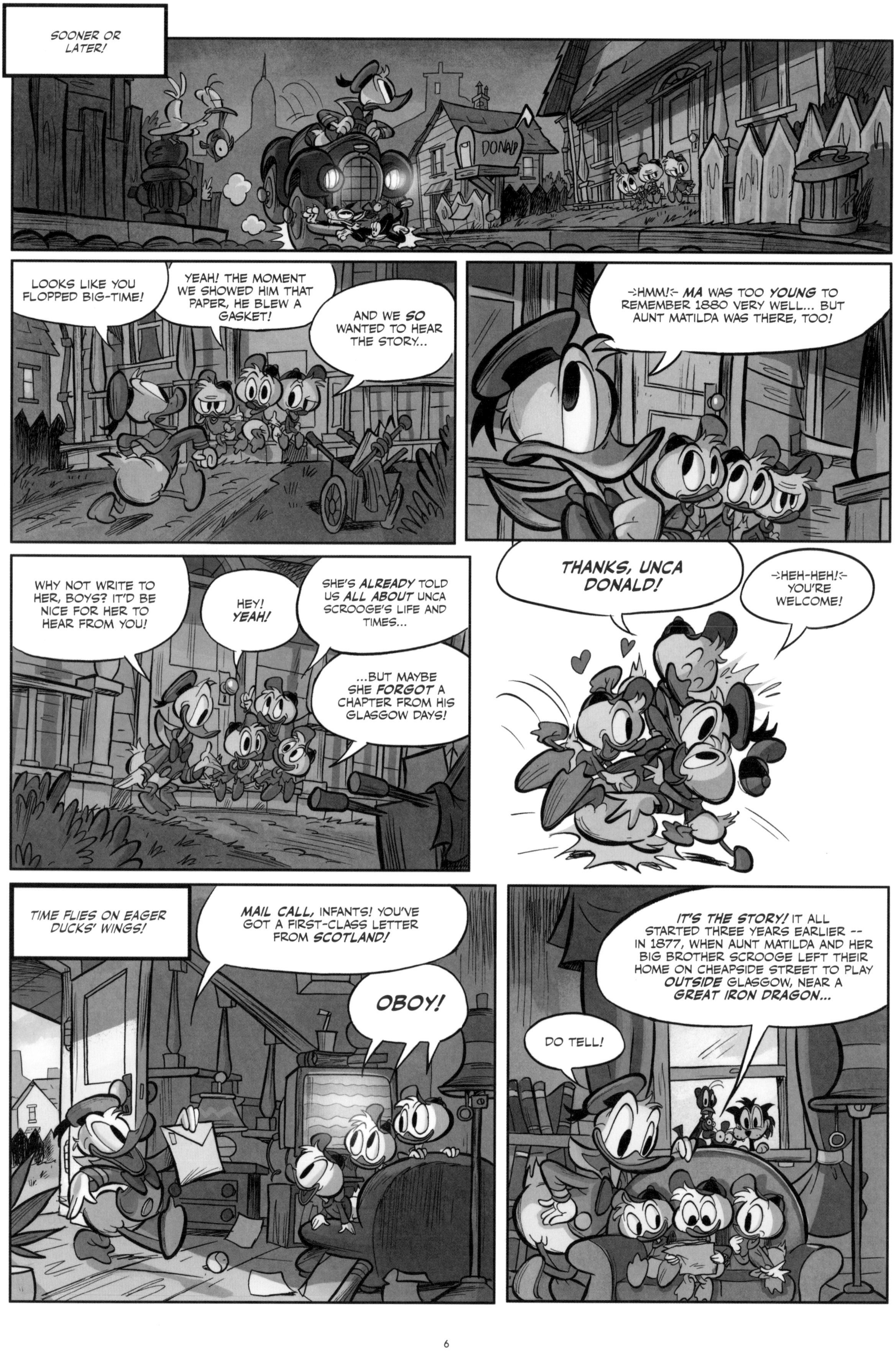
SOONER OR LATER!
DONALD
LOOKS LIKE YOU FLOPPED BIG-TIME!
YEAH! THE MOMENT WE SHOWED HIM THAT PAPER, HE BLEW A GASKET!
AND WE SO WANTED TO HEAR THE STORY...
–HMM!– MA WAS TOO YOUNG TO REMEMBER 1880 VERY WELL... BUT AUNT MATILDA WAS THERE, TOO!
WHY NOT WRITE TO HER, BOYS? IT'D BE NICE FOR HER TO HEAR FROM YOU!
HEY! YEAH!
SHE'S ALREADY TOLD US ALL ABOUT UNCA SCROOGE'S LIFE AND TIMES...
...BUT MAYBE SHE FORGOT A CHAPTER FROM HIS GLASGOW DAYS!
THANKS, UNCA DONALD!
–HEH-HEH!– YOU'RE WELCOME!
TIME FLIES ON EAGER DUCKS' WINGS!
MAIL CALL, INFANTS! YOU'VE GOT A FIRST-CLASS LETTER FROM SCOTLAND!
OBOY!
IT'S THE STORY! IT ALL STARTED THREE YEARS EARLIER -- IN 1877, WHEN AUNT MATILDA AND HER BIG BROTHER SCROOGE LEFT THEIR HOME ON CHEAPSIDE STREET TO PLAY OUTSIDE GLASGOW, NEAR A GREAT IRON DRAGON...
DO TELL!

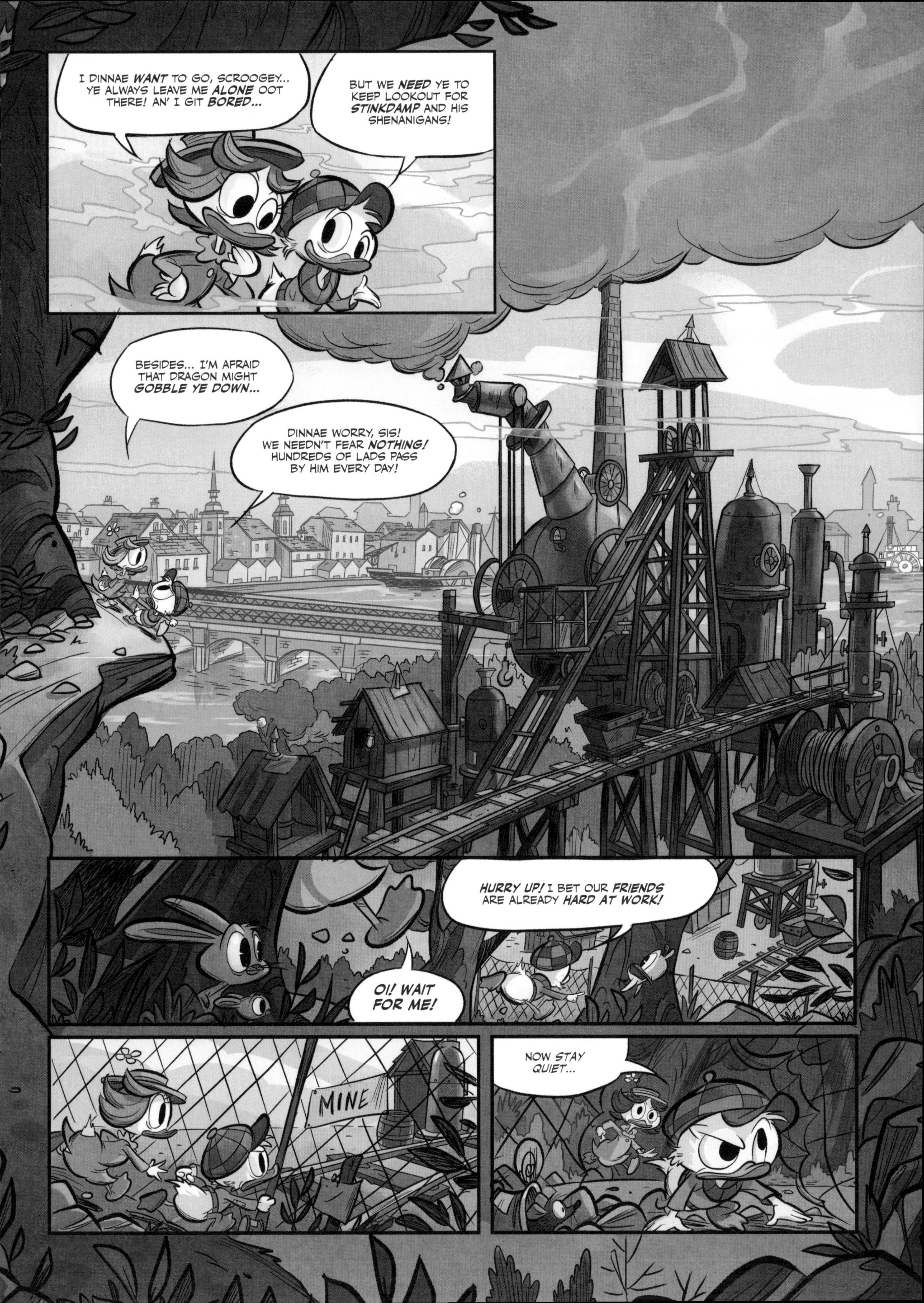
I DINNAE WANT TO GO, SCROOGEY... YE ALWAYS LEAVE ME ALONE OOT THERE! AN' I GIT BORED...
BUT WE NEED YE TO KEEP LOOKOUT FOR STINKDAMP AND HIS SHENANIGANS!
BESIDES... I'M AFRAID THAT DRAGON MIGHT GOBBLE YE DOWN...
DINNAE WORRY, SIS! WE NEEDN'T FEAR NOTHING! HUNDREDS OF LADS PASS BY HIM EVERY DAY!
HURRY UP! I BET OUR FRIENDS ARE ALREADY HARD AT WORK!
OI! WAIT FOR ME!
MINE
NOW STAY QUIET...

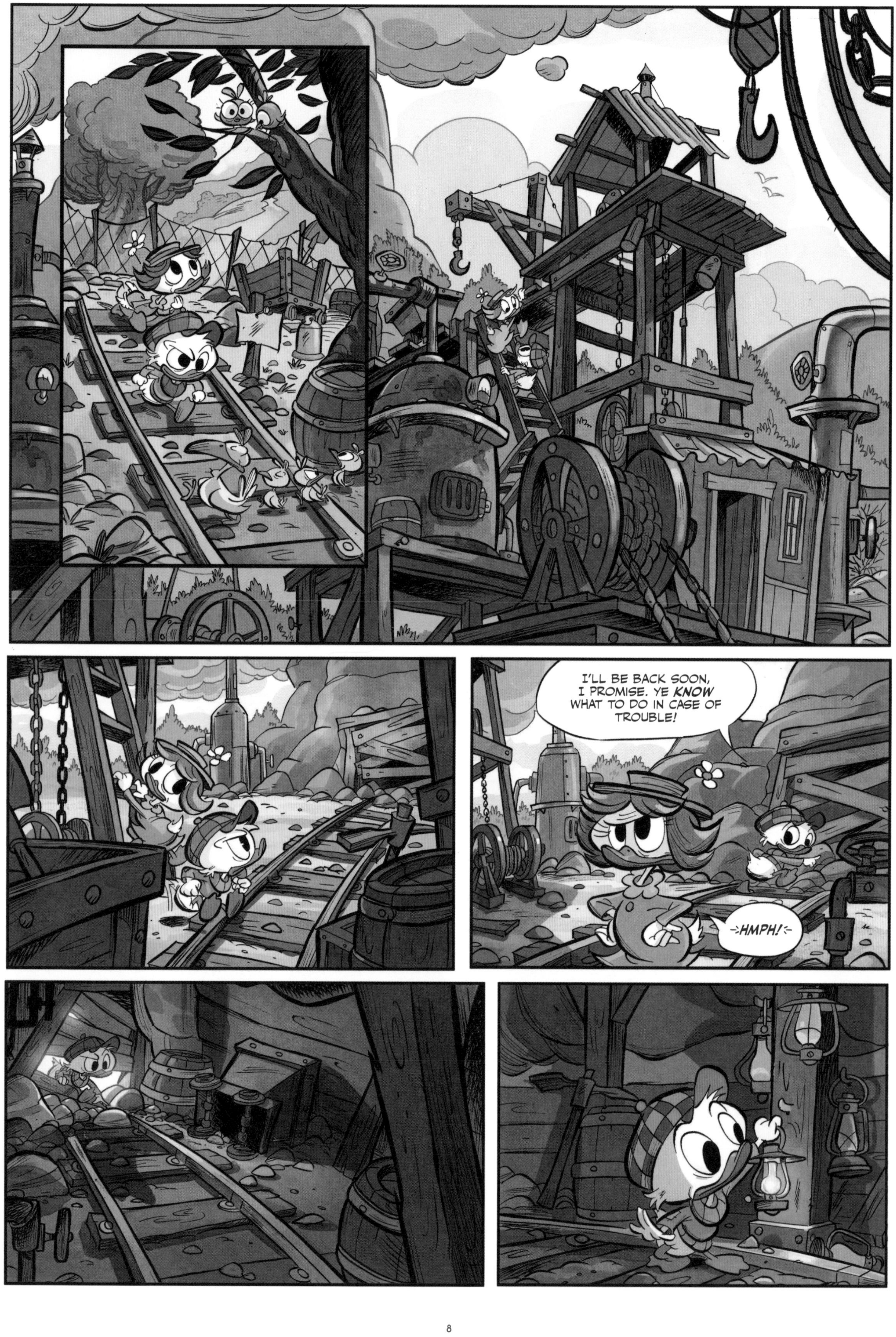
I'LL BE BACK SOON, I PROMISE. YE KNOW WHAT TO DO IN CASE OF TROUBLE!
-HMPH!-

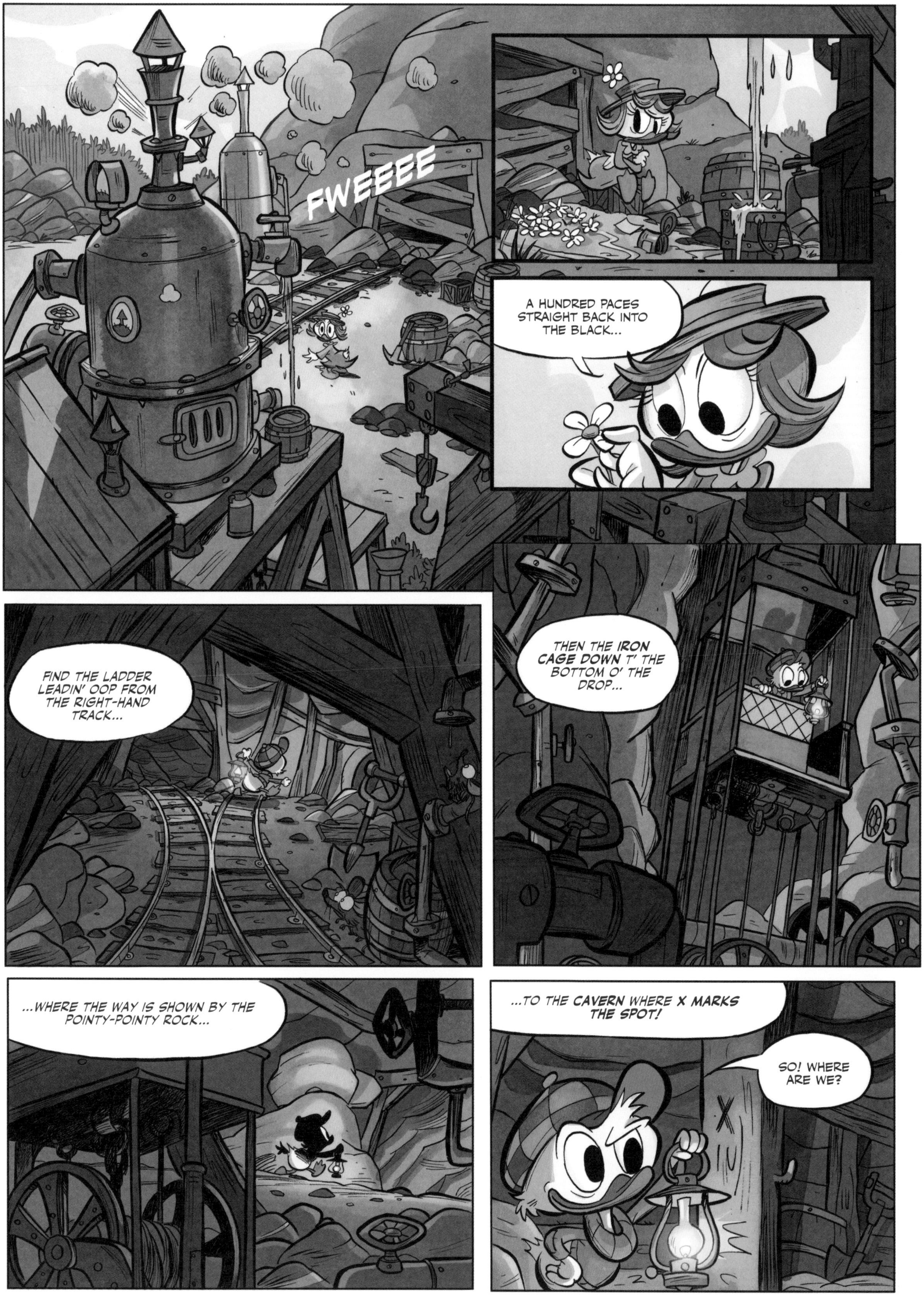
FWEEEE
A HUNDRED PACES STRAIGHT BACK INTO THE BLACK...
FIND THE LADDER LEADIN' OOP FROM THE RIGHT-HAND TRACK...
THEN THE IRON CAGE DOWN T' THE BOTTOM O' THE DROP...
...WHERE THE WAY IS SHOWN BY THE POINTY-POINTY ROCK...
...TO THE CAVERN WHERE X MARKS THE SPOT!
SO! WHERE ARE WE?
X

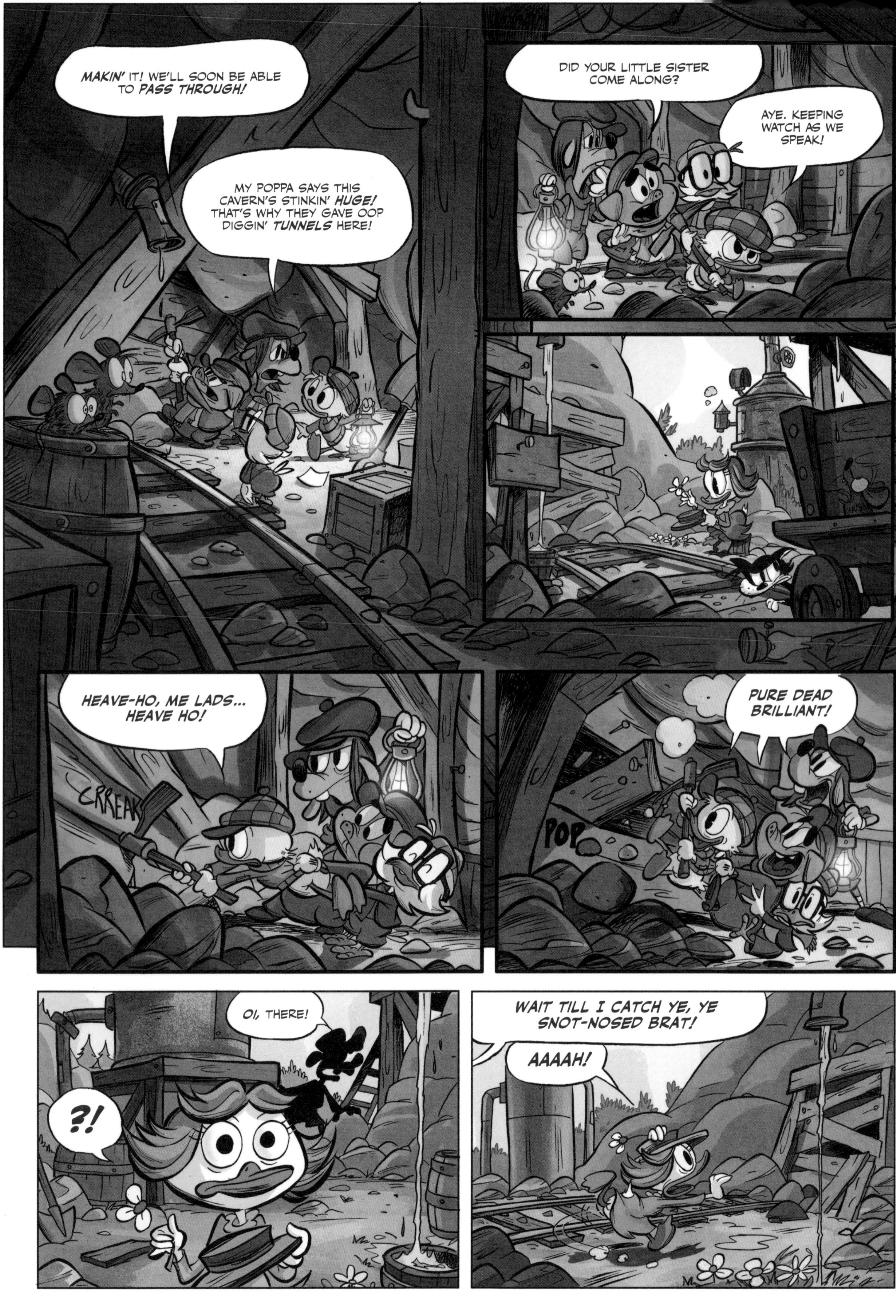

MAKIN' IT! WE'LL SOON BE ABLE TO PASS THROUGH!
MY POPPA SAYS THIS CAVERN'S STINKIN' HUGE! THAT'S WHY THEY GAVE OOP DIGGIN' TUNNELS HERE!
DID YOUR LITTLE SISTER COME ALONG?
AYE. KEEPING WATCH AS WE SPEAK!
HEAVE-HO, ME LADS... HEAVE HO!
CRREAK
PURE DEAD BRILLIANT!
POP
OI, THERE!
?!
WAIT TILL I CATCH YE, YE SNOT-NOSED BRAT!
AAAAH!

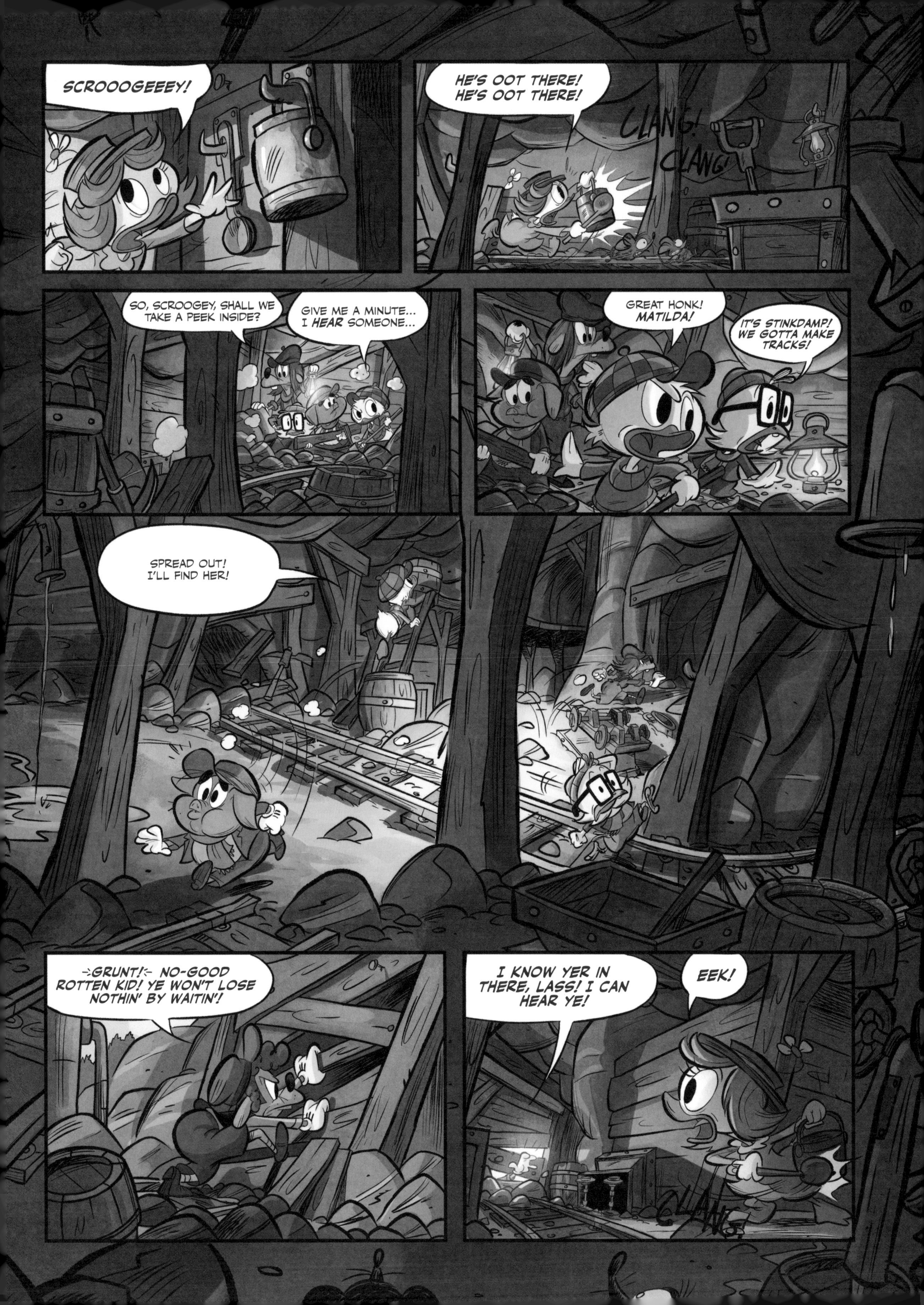
SCROOOGEEEY!
HE'S OOT THERE! HE'S OOT THERE!
CLANG! CLANG!
SO, SCROOGEY, SHALL WE TAKE A PEEK INSIDE?
GIVE ME A MINUTE... I HEAR SOMEONE...
GREAT HONK! MATILDA!
IT'S STINKDAMP! WE GOTTA MAKE TRACKS!
SPREAD OUT! I'LL FIND HER!
-GRUNT!- NO-GOOD ROTTEN KID! YE WON'T LOSE NOTHIN' BY WAITIN'!
I KNOW YER IN THERE, LASS! I CAN HEAR YE!
EEK!
CLANG

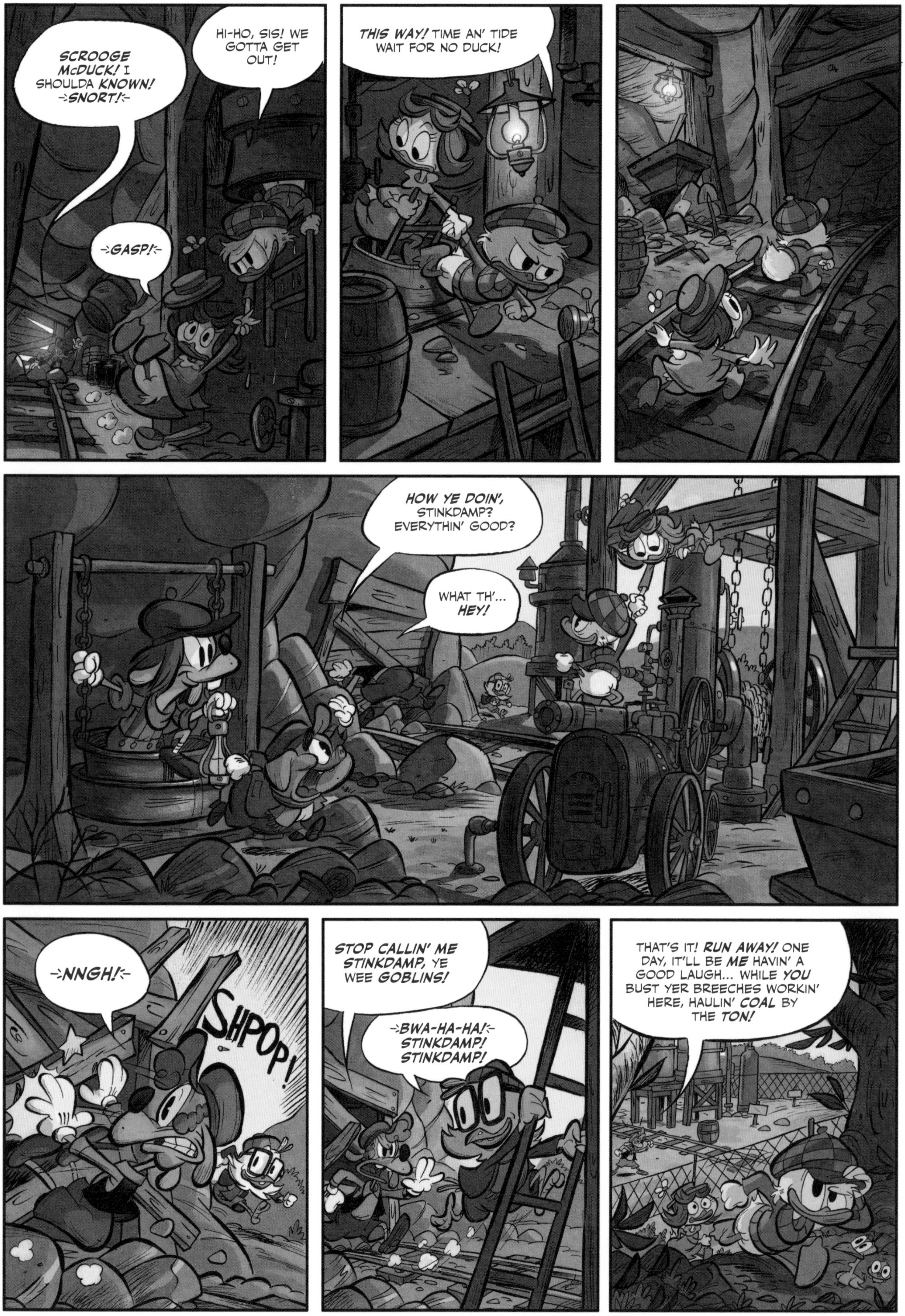
SCROOGE McDUCK! I SHOULDA KNOWN! -SNORT!-
HI-HO, SIS! WE GOTTA GET OUT!
-GASP!-
THIS WAY! TIME AN' TIDE WAIT FOR NO DUCK!
HOW YE DOIN', STINKDAMP? EVERYTHIN' GOOD?
WHAT TH'... HEY!
-NNGH!-
SHPOP!
STOP CALLIN' ME STINKDAMP, YE WEE GOBLINS!
-BWA-HA-HA!- STINKDAMP! STINKDAMP!
THAT'S IT! RUN AWAY! ONE DAY, IT'LL BE ME HAVIN' A GOOD LAUGH... WHILE YOU BUST YER BREECHES WORKIN' HERE, HAULIN' COAL BY THE TON!

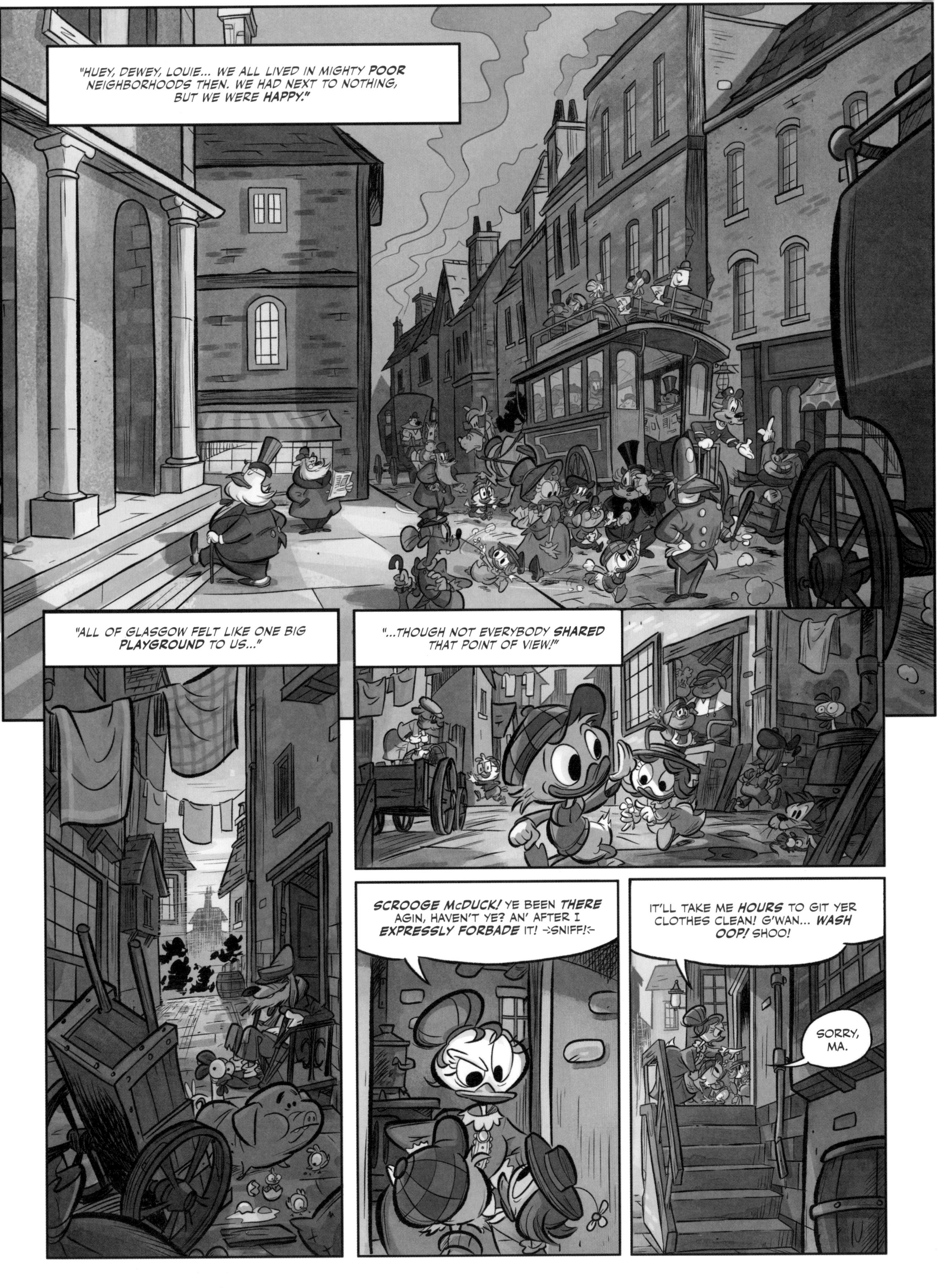
"HUEY, DEWEY, LOUIE... WE ALL LIVED IN MIGHTY POOR NEIGHBORHOODS THEN. WE HAD NEXT TO NOTHING, BUT WE WERE HAPPY."
"ALL OF GLASGOW FELT LIKE ONE BIG PLAYGROUND TO US..."
"...THOUGH NOT EVERYBODY SHARED THAT POINT OF VIEW!"
SCROOGE McDUCK! YE BEEN THERE AGIN, HAVEN'T YE? AN' AFTER I EXPRESSLY FORBADE IT! -SNIFF!-
IT'LL TAKE ME HOURS TO GIT YER CLOTHES CLEAN! G'WAN... WASH OOP! SHOO!
SORRY, MA.

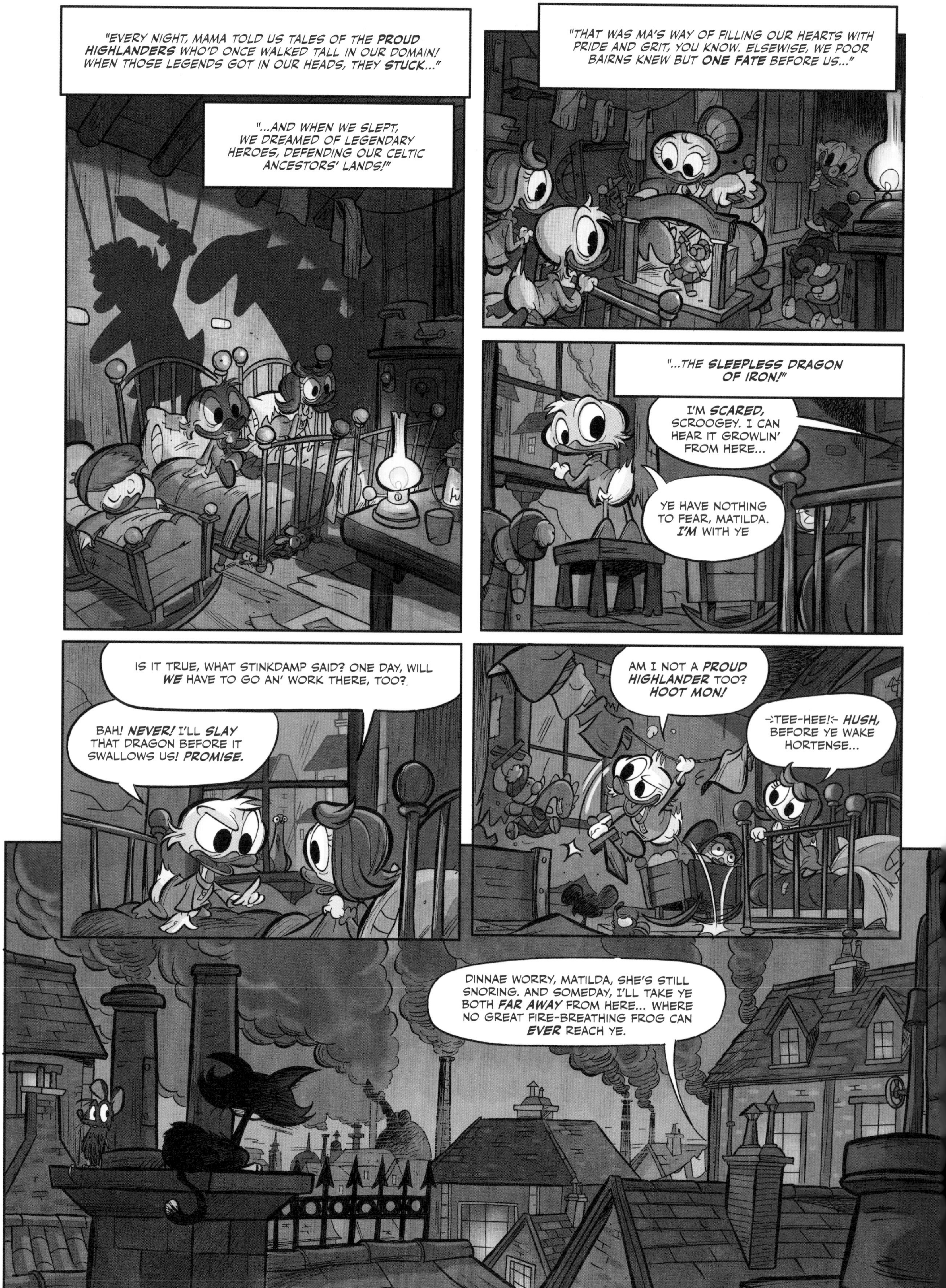
"EVERY NIGHT, MAMA TOLD US TALES OF THE PROUD HIGHLANDERS WHO'D ONCE WALKED TALL IN OUR DOMAIN! WHEN THOSE LEGENDS GOT IN OUR HEADS, THEY STUCK..."
"...AND WHEN WE SLEPT, WE DREAMED OF LEGENDARY HEROES, DEFENDING OUR CELTIC ANCESTORS' LANDS!"
"THAT WAS MA'S WAY OF FILLING OUR HEARTS WITH PRIDE AND GRIT, YOU KNOW. ELSEWISE, WE POOR BAIRNS KNEW BUT ONE FATE BEFORE US..."
"...THE SLEEPLESS DRAGON OF IRON!"
I'M SCARED, SCROOGEY. I CAN HEAR IT GROWLIN' FROM HERE...
YE HAVE NOTHING TO FEAR, MATILDA. I'M WITH YE
IS IT TRUE, WHAT STINKDAMP SAID? ONE DAY, WILL WE HAVE TO GO AN' WORK THERE, TOO?
BAH! NEVER! I'LL SLAY THAT DRAGON BEFORE IT SWALLOWS US! PROMISE.
AM I NOT A PROUD HIGHLANDER TOO? HOOT MON!
-TEE-HEE!- HUSH, BEFORE YE WAKE HORTENSE...
DINNAE WORRY, MATILDA, SHE'S STILL SNORING. AND SOMEDAY, I'LL TAKE YE BOTH FAR AWAY FROM HERE... WHERE NO GREAT FIRE-BREATHING FROG CAN EVER REACH YE.

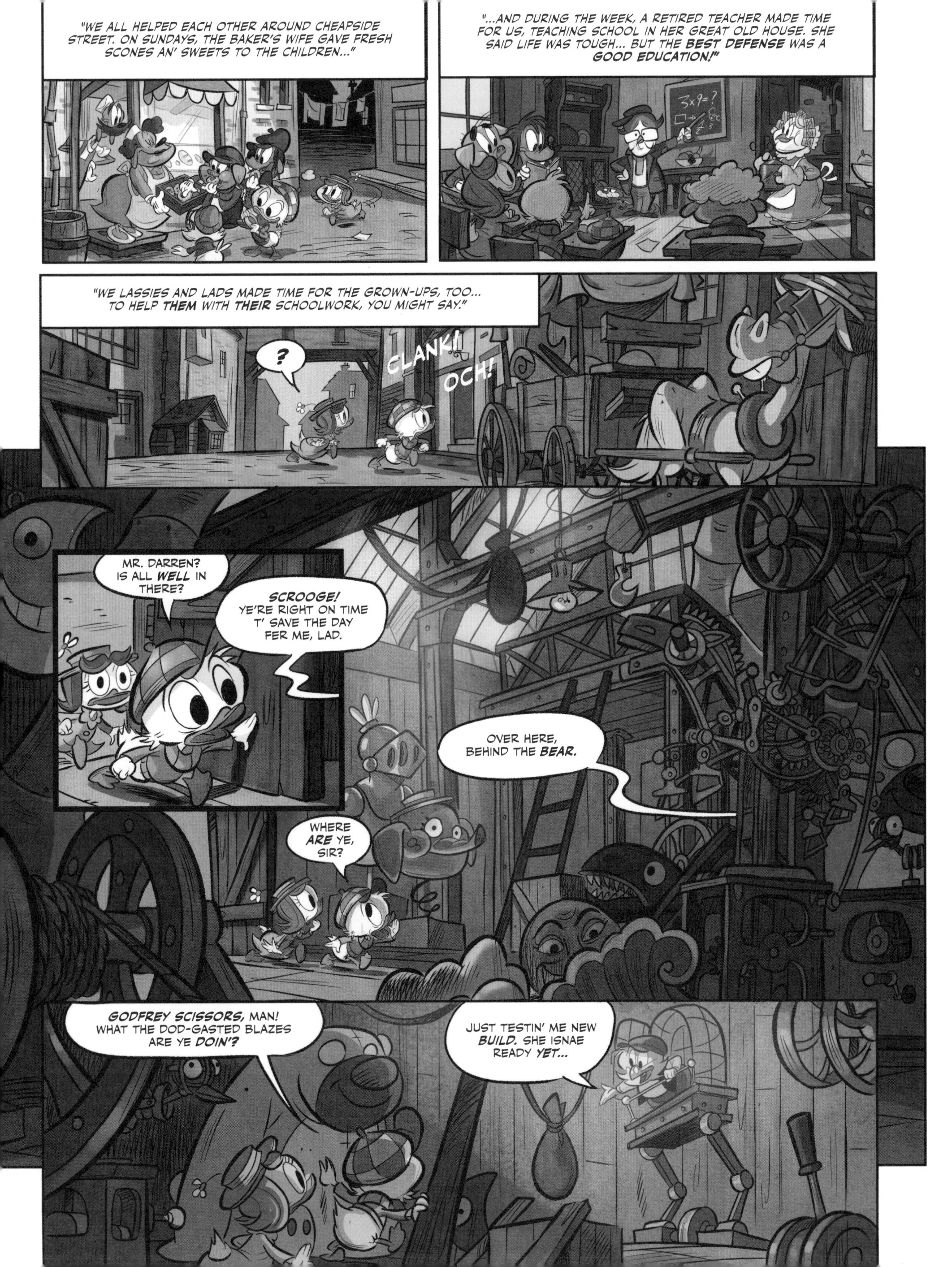
"WE ALL HELPED EACH OTHER AROUND CHEAPSIDE STREET. ON SUNDAYS, THE BAKER'S WIFE GAVE FRESH SCONES AN' SWEETS TO THE CHILDREN..."
"...AND DURING THE WEEK, A RETIRED TEACHER MADE TIME FOR US, TEACHING SCHOOL IN HER GREAT OLD HOUSE. SHE SAID LIFE WAS TOUGH... BUT THE BEST DEFENSE WAS A GOOD EDUCATION!"
3x9=?
"WE LASSIES AND LADS MADE TIME FOR THE GROWN-UPS, TOO... TO HELP THEM WITH THEIR SCHOOLWORK, YOU MIGHT SAY."
?
CLANK!
OCH!
MR. DARREN? IS ALL WELL IN THERE?
SCROOGE! YE'RE RIGHT ON TIME T' SAVE THE DAY FER ME, LAD.
OVER HERE, BEHIND THE BEAR.
WHERE ARE YE, SIR?
GODFREY SCISSORS, MAN! WHAT THE DOD-GASTED BLAZES ARE YE DOIN'?
JUST TESTIN' ME NEW BUILD. SHE ISNAE READY YET...

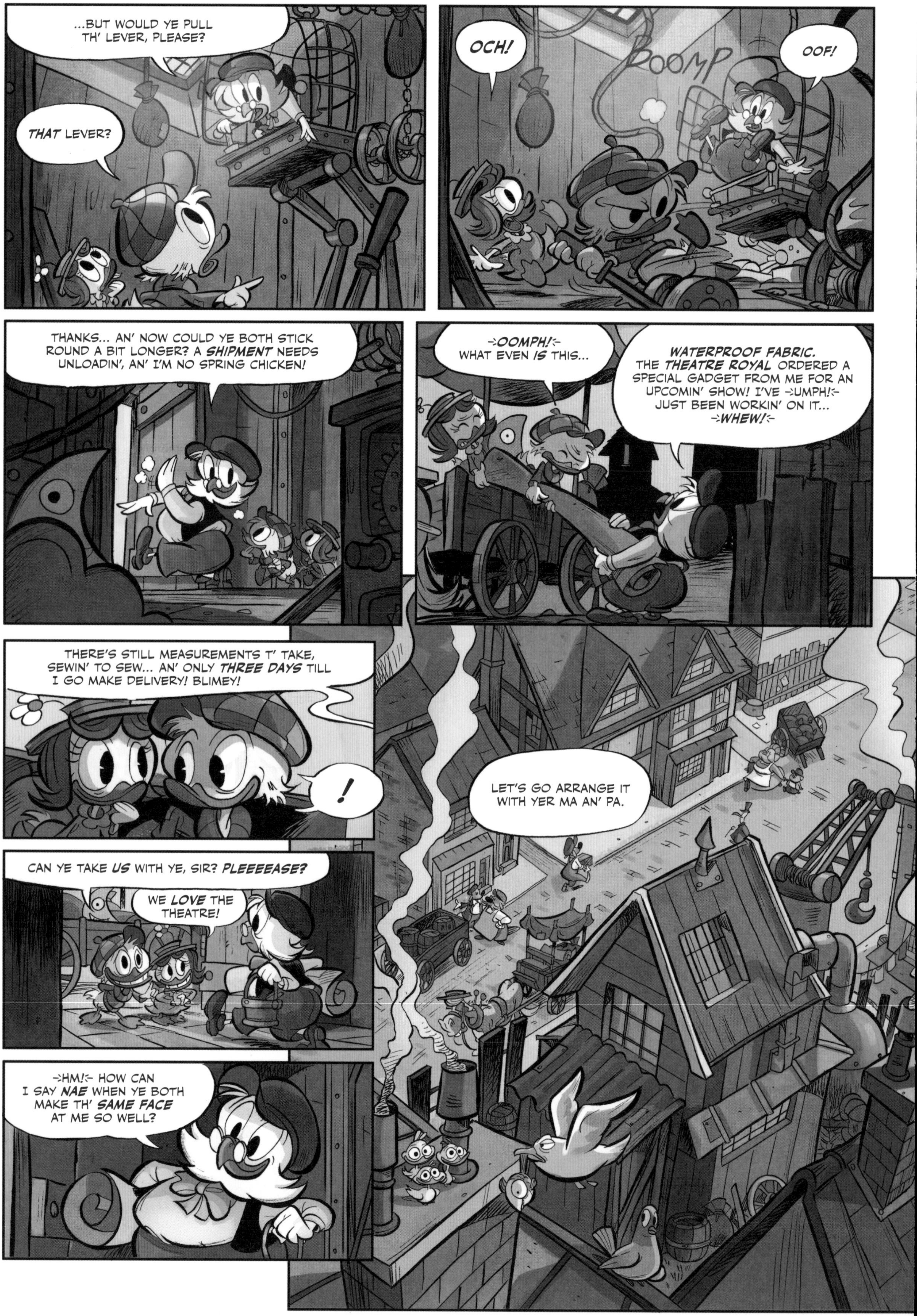
...BUT WOULD YE PULL TH' LEVER, PLEASE?
THAT LEVER?
OCH!
BOOMP
OOF!
THANKS... AN' NOW COULD YE BOTH STICK ROUND A BIT LONGER? A SHIPMENT NEEDS UNLOADIN', AN' I'M NO SPRING CHICKEN!
-OOMPH!- WHAT EVEN IS THIS...
WATERPROOF FABRIC. THE THEATRE ROYAL ORDERED A SPECIAL GADGET FROM ME FOR AN UPCOMIN' SHOW! I'VE -UMPH!- JUST BEEN WORKIN' ON IT... -WHEW!-
THERE'S STILL MEASUREMENTS T' TAKE, SEWIN' TO SEW... AN' ONLY THREE DAYS TILL I GO MAKE DELIVERY! BLIMEY!
!
CAN YE TAKE US WITH YE, SIR? PLEEEEASE?
WE LOVE THE THEATRE!
-HM!- HOW CAN I SAY NAE WHEN YE BOTH MAKE TH' SAME FACE AT ME SO WELL?
LET'S GO ARRANGE IT WITH YER MA AN' PA.

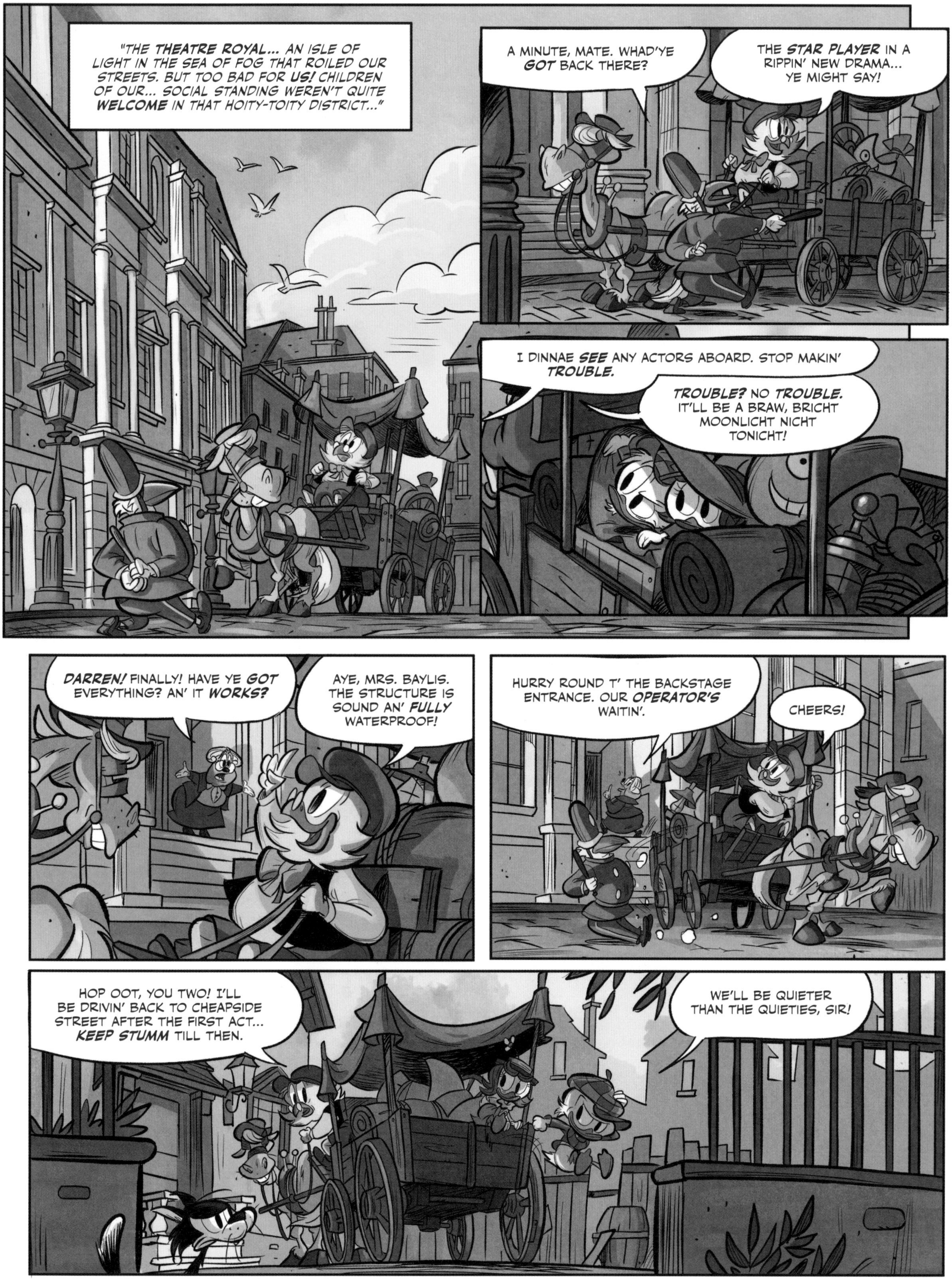
"THE THEATRE ROYAL... AN ISLE OF LIGHT IN THE SEA OF FOG THAT ROILED OUR STREETS. BUT TOO BAD FOR US! CHILDREN OF OUR... SOCIAL STANDING WEREN'T QUITE WELCOME IN THAT HOITY-TOITY DISTRICT..."
A MINUTE, MATE. WHAD'YE GOT BACK THERE?
THE STAR PLAYER IN A RIPPIN' NEW DRAMA... YE MIGHT SAY!
I DINNAE SEE ANY ACTORS ABOARD. STOP MAKIN' TROUBLE.
TROUBLE? NO TROUBLE. IT'LL BE A BRAW, BRICHT MOONLICHT NICHT TONICHT!
DARREN! FINALLY! HAVE YE GOT EVERYTHING? AN' IT WORKS?
AYE, MRS. BAYLIS. THE STRUCTURE IS SOUND AN' FULLY WATERPROOF!
HURRY ROUND T' THE BACKSTAGE ENTRANCE. OUR OPERATOR'S WAITIN'.
CHEERS!
HOP OOT, YOU TWO! I'LL BE DRIVIN' BACK TO CHEAPSIDE STREET AFTER THE FIRST ACT... KEEP STUMM TILL THEN.
WE'LL BE QUIETER THAN THE QUIETIES, SIR!

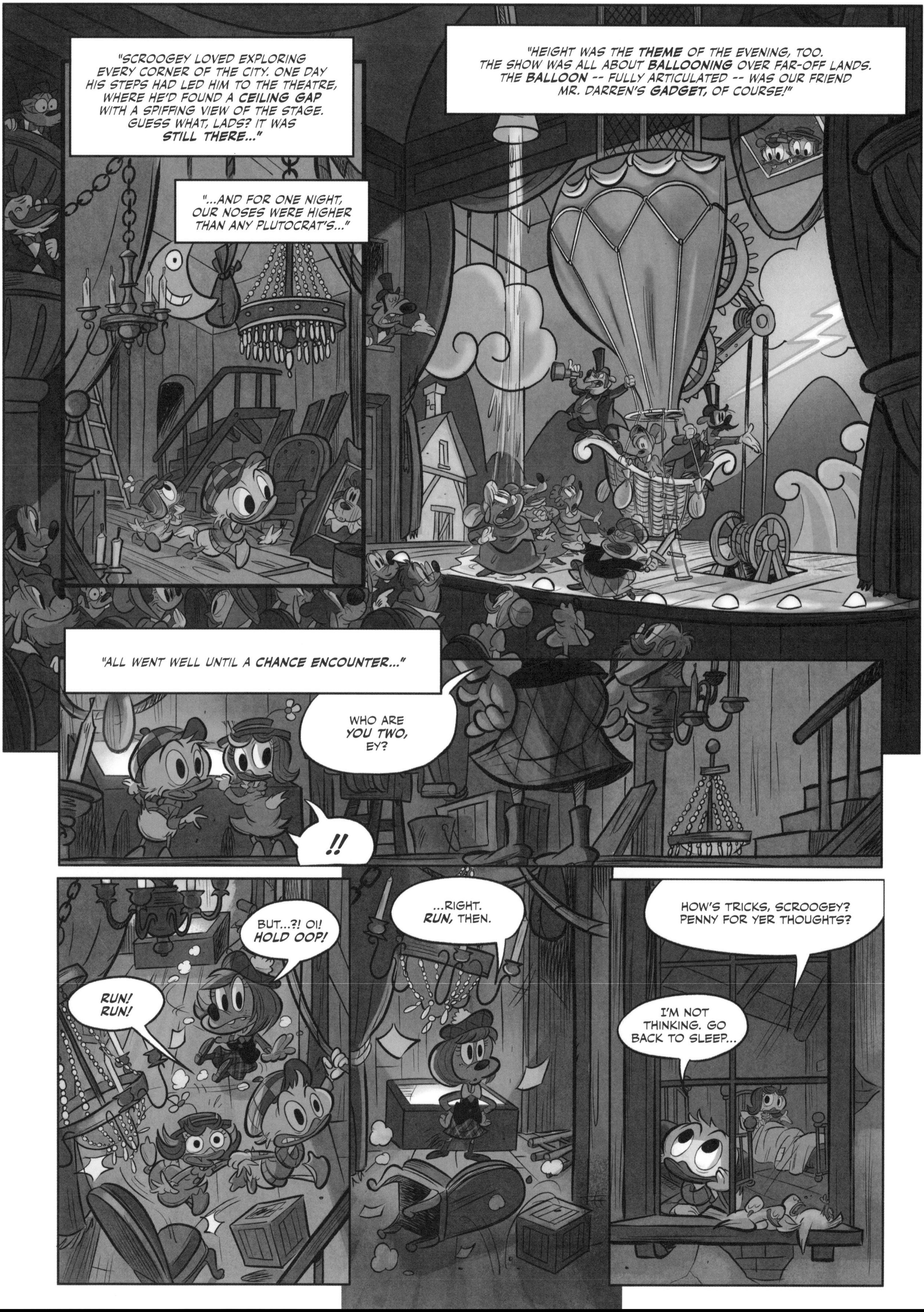
"SCROOGEY LOVED EXPLORING EVERY CORNER OF THE CITY. ONE DAY HIS STEPS HAD LED HIM TO THE THEATRE, WHERE HE'D FOUND A CEILING GAP WITH A SPIFFING VIEW OF THE STAGE. GUESS WHAT, LADS? IT WAS STILL THERE..."
"...AND FOR ONE NIGHT, OUR NOSES WERE HIGHER THAN ANY PLUTOCRAT'S..."
"HEIGHT WAS THE THEME OF THE EVENING, TOO. THE SHOW WAS ALL ABOUT BALLOONING OVER FAR-OFF LANDS. THE BALLOON -- FULLY ARTICULATED -- WAS OUR FRIEND MR. DARREN'S GADGET, OF COURSE!"
"ALL WENT WELL UNTIL A CHANCE ENCOUNTER..."
WHO ARE YOU TWO, EY?
!!
BUT...?! OI! HOLD OOP!
RUN! RUN!
...RIGHT. RUN, THEN.
HOW'S TRICKS, SCROOGEY? PENNY FOR YER THOUGHTS?
I'M NOT THINKING. GO BACK TO SLEEP...

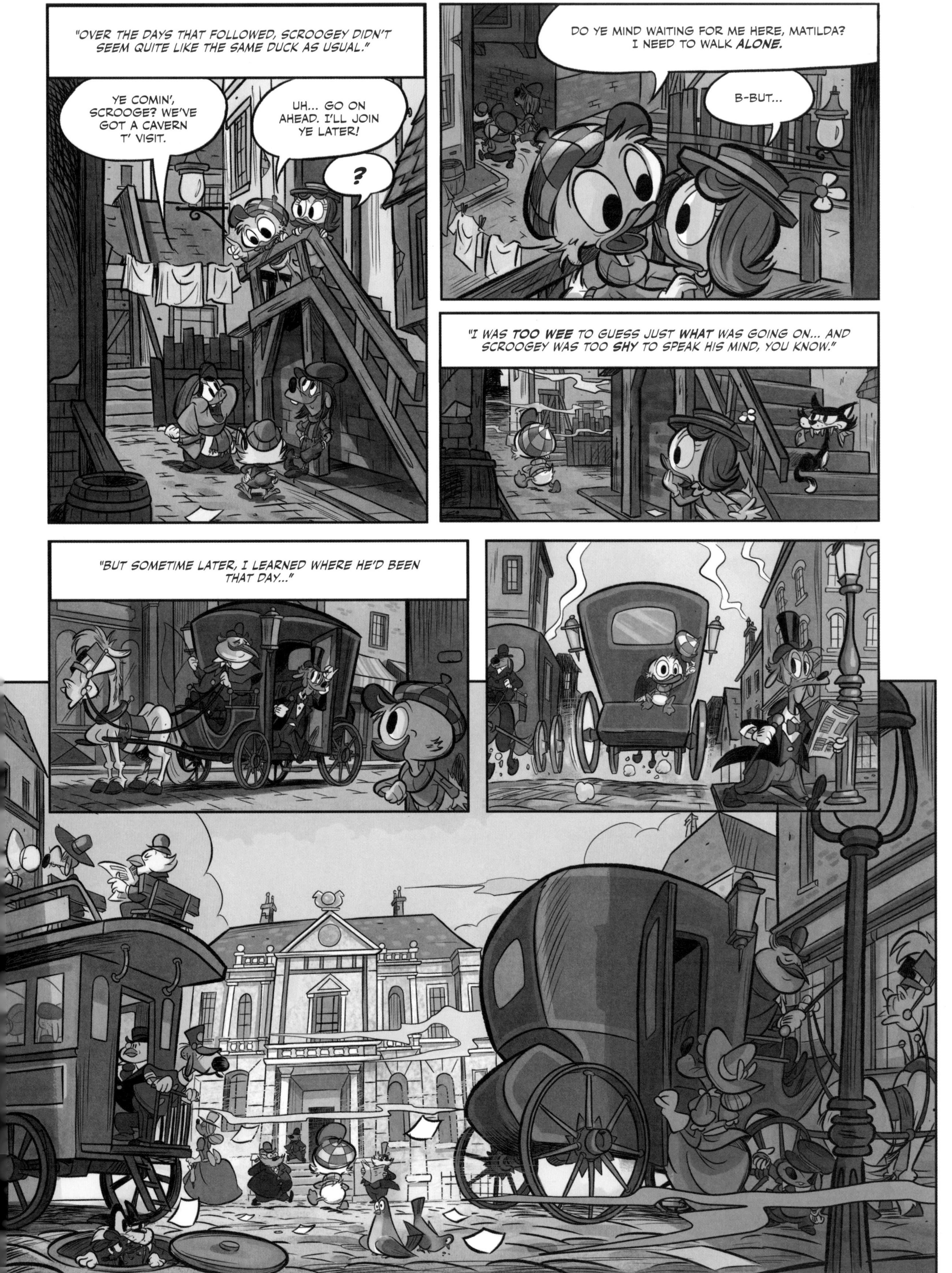
"OVER THE DAYS THAT FOLLOWED, SCROOGEY DIDN'T SEEM QUITE LIKE THE SAME DUCK AS USUAL."
YE COMIN', SCROOGE? WE'VE GOT A CAVERN T' VISIT.
UH... GO ON AHEAD. I'LL JOIN YE LATER!
?
DO YE MIND WAITING FOR ME HERE, MATILDA? I NEED TO WALK ALONE.
B-BUT...
"I WAS TOO WEE TO GUESS JUST WHAT WAS GOING ON... AND SCROOGEY WAS TOO SHY TO SPEAK HIS MIND, YOU KNOW."
"BUT SOMETIME LATER, I LEARNED WHERE HE'D BEEN THAT DAY..."

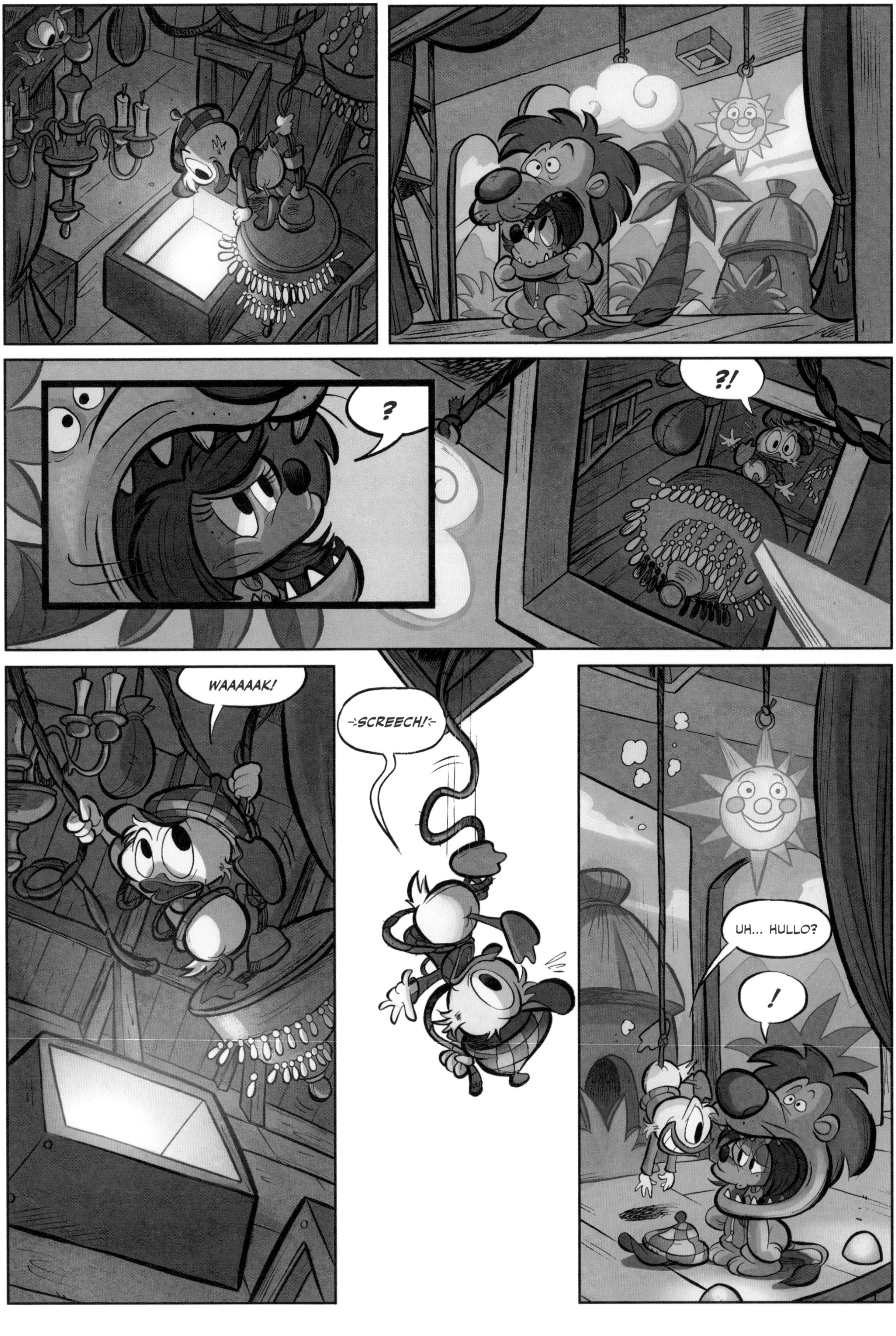
?
?!
WAAAAAK!
SCREECH!
UH... HULLO?
!

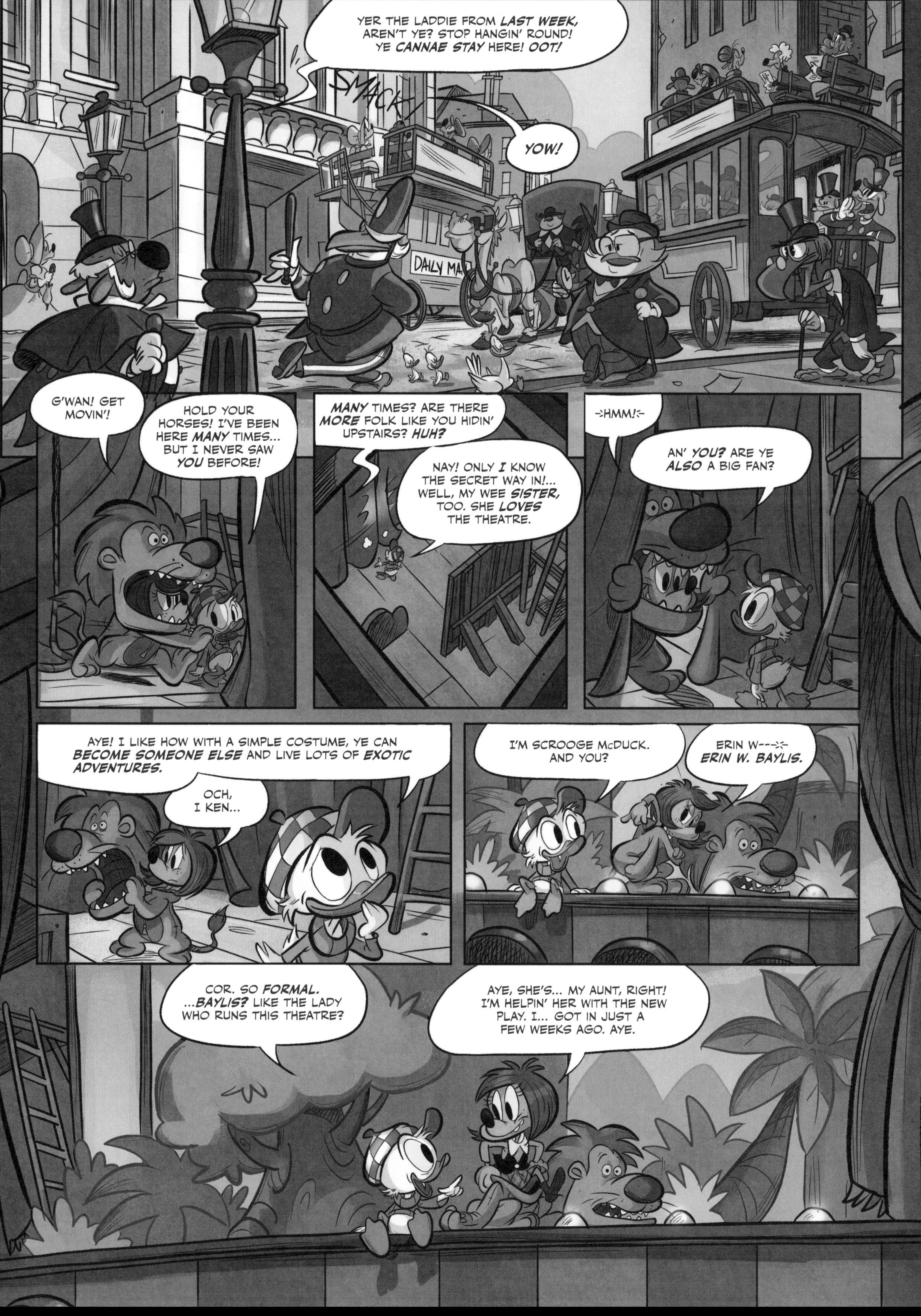
YER THE LADDIE FROM LAST WEEK, AREN'T YE? STOP HANGIN' ROUND! YE CANNAE STAY HERE! OOT!
SMACK!
YOW!
DAILY MA
G'WAN! GET MOVIN'!
HOLD YOUR HORSES! I'VE BEEN HERE MANY TIMES... BUT I NEVER SAW YOU BEFORE!
MANY TIMES? ARE THERE MORE FOLK LIKE YOU HIDIN' UPSTAIRS? HUH?
NAY! ONLY I KNOW THE SECRET WAY IN!... WELL, MY WEE SISTER, TOO. SHE LOVES THE THEATRE.
HMM!
AN' YOU? ARE YE ALSO A BIG FAN?
AYE! I LIKE HOW WITH A SIMPLE COSTUME, YE CAN BECOME SOMEONE ELSE AND LIVE LOTS OF EXOTIC ADVENTURES.
OCH, I KEN...
I'M SCROOGE McDUCK. AND YOU?
ERIN W---
ERIN W. BAYLIS.
COR. SO FORMAL. ...BAYLIS? LIKE THE LADY WHO RUNS THIS THEATRE?
AYE, SHE'S... MY AUNT, RIGHT! I'M HELPIN' HER WITH THE NEW PLAY. I... GOT IN JUST A FEW WEEKS AGO. AYE.

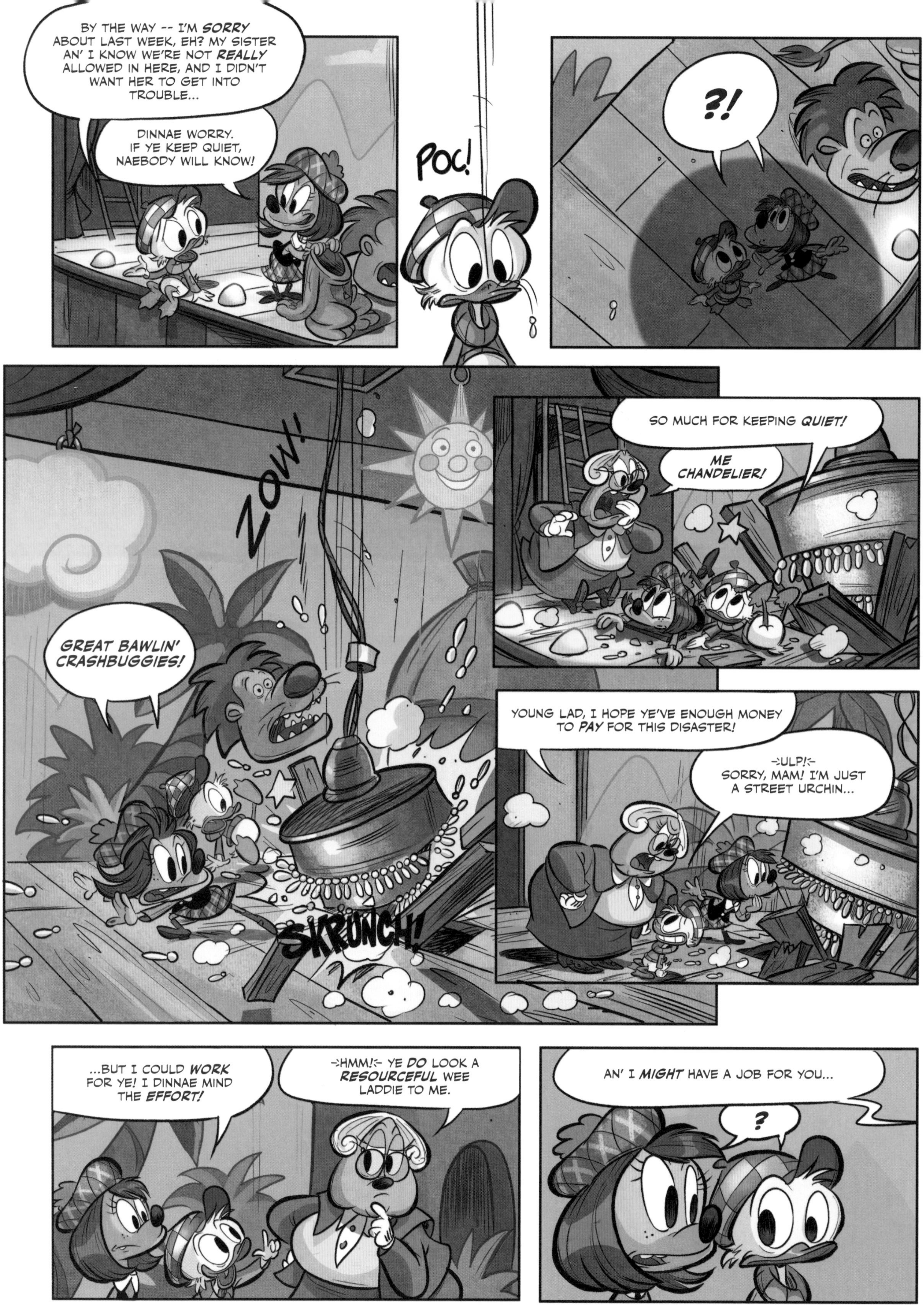

BY THE WAY -- I'M SORRY ABOUT LAST WEEK, EH? MY SISTER AN' I KNOW WE'RE NOT REALLY ALLOWED IN HERE, AND I DIDN'T WANT HER TO GET INTO TROUBLE...
DINNAE WORRY. IF YE KEEP QUIET, NAEBODY WILL KNOW!
POC!
?!
ZOW!
GREAT BAWLIN' CRASHBUGGIES!
SKRUNCH!
SO MUCH FOR KEEPING QUIET!
ME CHANDELIER!
YOUNG LAD, I HOPE YE'VE ENOUGH MONEY TO PAY FOR THIS DISASTER!
-ULP!- SORRY, MAM! I'M JUST A STREET URCHIN...
...BUT I COULD WORK FOR YE! I DINNAE MIND THE EFFORT!
-HMM!- YE DO LOOK A RESOURCEFUL WEE LADDIE TO ME.
AN' I MIGHT HAVE A JOB FOR YOU...
?

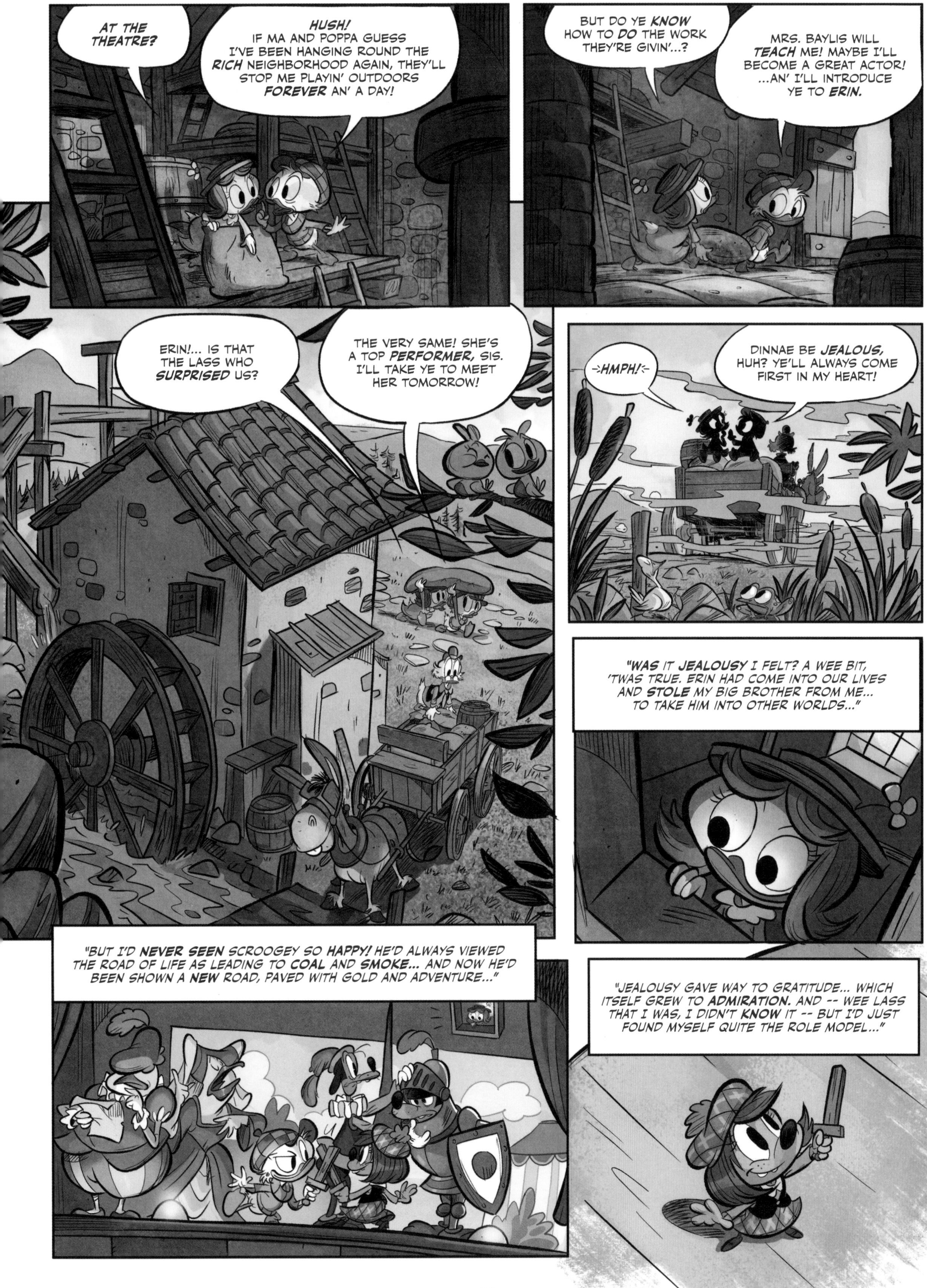

AT THE THEATRE?
HUSH! IF MA AND POPPA GUESS I'VE BEEN HANGING ROUND THE RICH NEIGHBORHOOD AGAIN, THEY'LL STOP ME PLAYIN' OUTDOORS FOREVER AN' A DAY!
BUT DO YE KNOW HOW TO DO THE WORK THEY'RE GIVIN'...?
MRS. BAYLIS WILL TEACH ME! MAYBE I'LL BECOME A GREAT ACTOR! ...AN' I'LL INTRODUCE YE TO ERIN.
ERIN!... IS THAT THE LASS WHO SURPRISED US?
THE VERY SAME! SHE'S A TOP PERFORMER, SIS. I'LL TAKE YE TO MEET HER TOMORROW!
HMPH!
DINNAE BE JEALOUS, HUH? YE'LL ALWAYS COME FIRST IN MY HEART!
"WAS IT JEALOUSY I FELT? A WEE BIT, 'TWAS TRUE. ERIN HAD COME INTO OUR LIVES AND STOLE MY BIG BROTHER FROM ME... TO TAKE HIM INTO OTHER WORLDS..."
"BUT I'D NEVER SEEN SCROOGEY SO HAPPY! HE'D ALWAYS VIEWED THE ROAD OF LIFE AS LEADING TO COAL AND SMOKE... AND NOW HE'D BEEN SHOWN A NEW ROAD, PAVED WITH GOLD AND ADVENTURE..."
"JEALOUSY GAVE WAY TO GRATITUDE... WHICH ITSELF GREW TO ADMIRATION. AND -- WEE LASS THAT I WAS, I DIDN'T KNOW IT -- BUT I'D JUST FOUND MYSELF QUITE THE ROLE MODEL..."

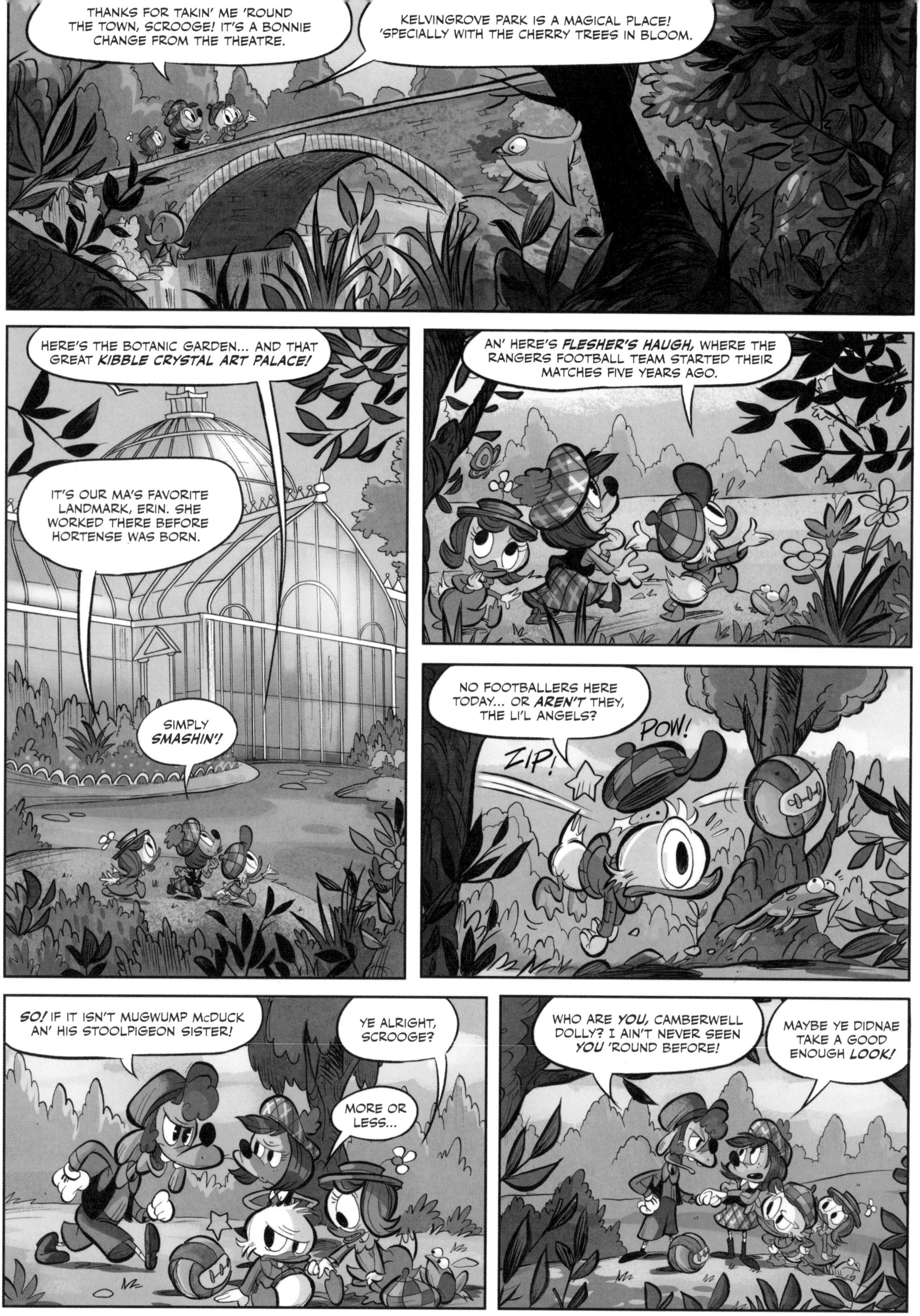
THANKS FOR TAKIN' ME 'ROUND THE TOWN, SCROOGE! IT'S A BONNIE CHANGE FROM THE THEATRE.
KELVINGROVE PARK IS A MAGICAL PLACE! 'SPECIALLY WITH THE CHERRY TREES IN BLOOM.
HERE'S THE BOTANIC GARDEN... AND THAT GREAT KIBBLE CRYSTAL ART PALACE!
IT'S OUR MA'S FAVORITE LANDMARK, ERIN. SHE WORKED THERE BEFORE HORTENSE WAS BORN.
SIMPLY SMASHIN'!
AN' HERE'S FLESHER'S HAUGH, WHERE THE RANGERS FOOTBALL TEAM STARTED THEIR MATCHES FIVE YEARS AGO.
NO FOOTBALLERS HERE TODAY... OR AREN'T THEY, THE LI'L ANGELS?
POW!
ZIP!
SO! IF IT ISN'T MUGWUMP McDUCK AN' HIS STOOLPIGEON SISTER!
YE ALRIGHT, SCROOGE?
MORE OR LESS...
WHO ARE YOU, CAMBERWELL DOLLY? I AIN'T NEVER SEEN YOU 'ROUND BEFORE!
MAYBE YE DIDNAE TAKE A GOOD ENOUGH LOOK!

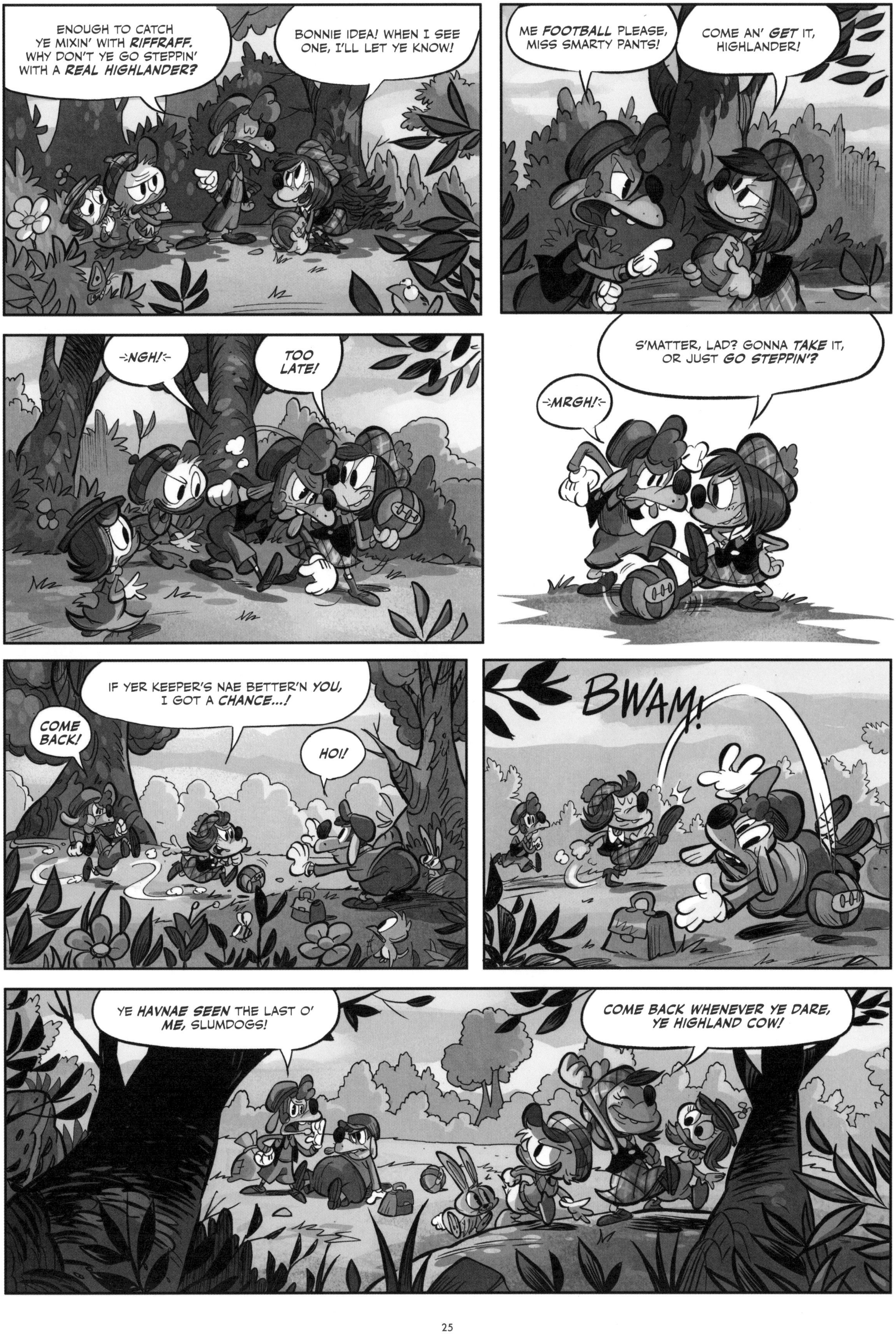
ENOUGH TO CATCH YE MIXIN' WITH RIFFRAFF. WHY DON'T YE GO STEPPIN' WITH A REAL HIGHLANDER?
BONNIE IDEA! WHEN I SEE ONE, I'LL LET YE KNOW!
ME FOOTBALL PLEASE, MISS SMARTY PANTS!
COME AN' GET IT, HIGHLANDER!
-NGH!-
TOO LATE!
S'MATTER, LAD? GONNA TAKE IT, OR JUST GO STEPPIN'?
-MRGH!-
IF YER KEEPER'S NAE BETTER'N YOU, I GOT A CHANCE...!
COME BACK!
HOI!
BWAM!
YE HAVNAE SEEN THE LAST O' ME, SLUMDOGS!
COME BACK WHENEVER YE DARE, YE HIGHLAND COW!

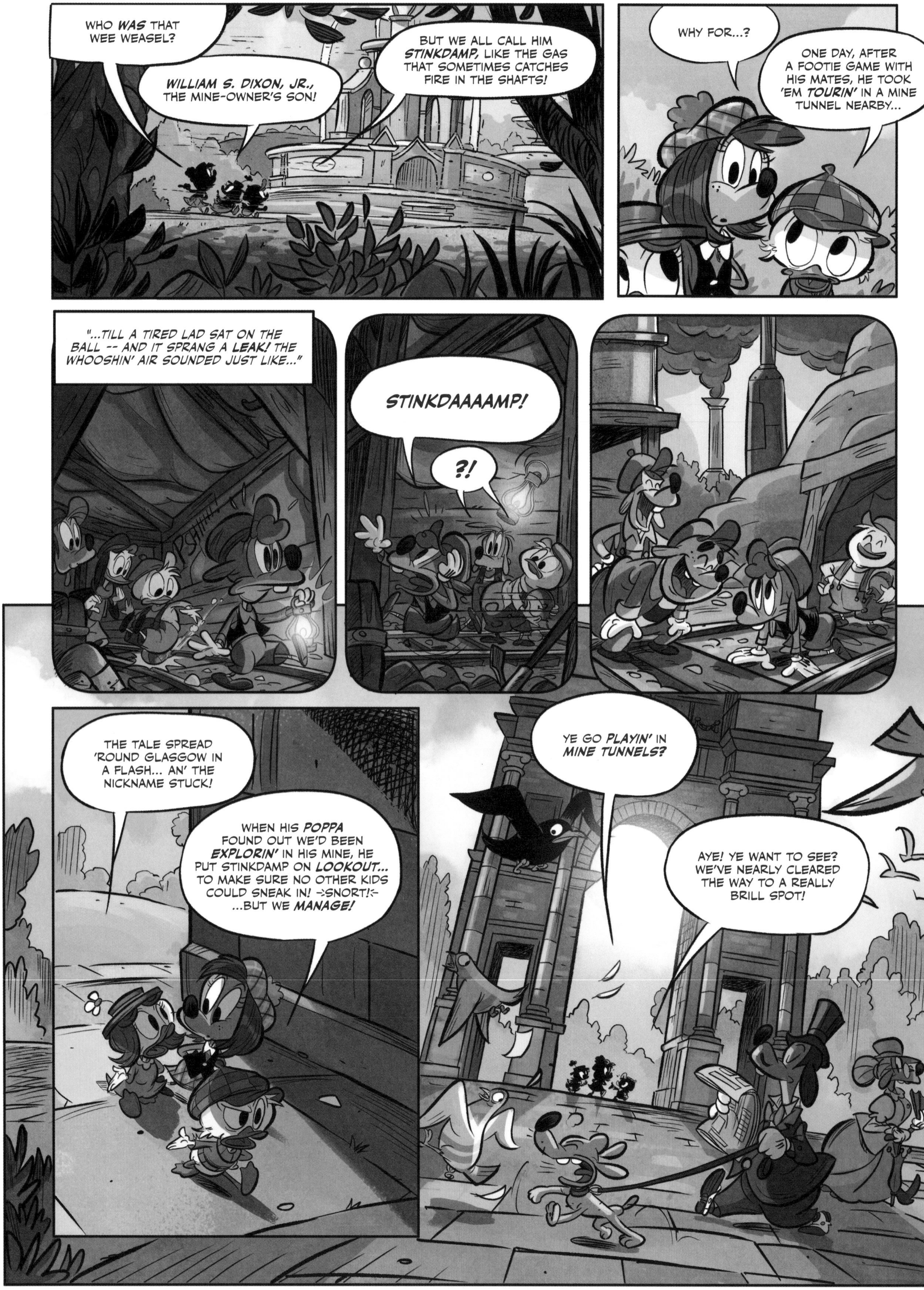
WHO WAS THAT WEE WEASEL?
WILLIAM S. DIXON, JR., THE MINE-OWNER'S SON!
BUT WE ALL CALL HIM STINKDAMP, LIKE THE GAS THAT SOMETIMES CATCHES FIRE IN THE SHAFTS!
WHY FOR...?
ONE DAY, AFTER A FOOTIE GAME WITH HIS MATES, HE TOOK 'EM TOURIN' IN A MINE TUNNEL NEARBY...
"...TILL A TIRED LAD SAT ON THE BALL -- AND IT SPRANG A LEAK! THE WHOOSHIN' AIR SOUNDED JUST LIKE..."
STINKDAAAAMP!
?!
THE TALE SPREAD 'ROUND GLASGOW IN A FLASH... AN' THE NICKNAME STUCK!
WHEN HIS POPPA FOUND OUT WE'D BEEN EXPLORIN' IN HIS MINE, HE PUT STINKDAMP ON LOOKOUT... TO MAKE SURE NO OTHER KIDS COULD SNEAK IN! ->SNORT!<- ...BUT WE MANAGE!
YE GO PLAYIN' IN MINE TUNNELS?
AYE! YE WANT TO SEE? WE'VE NEARLY CLEARED THE WAY TO A REALLY BRILL SPOT!

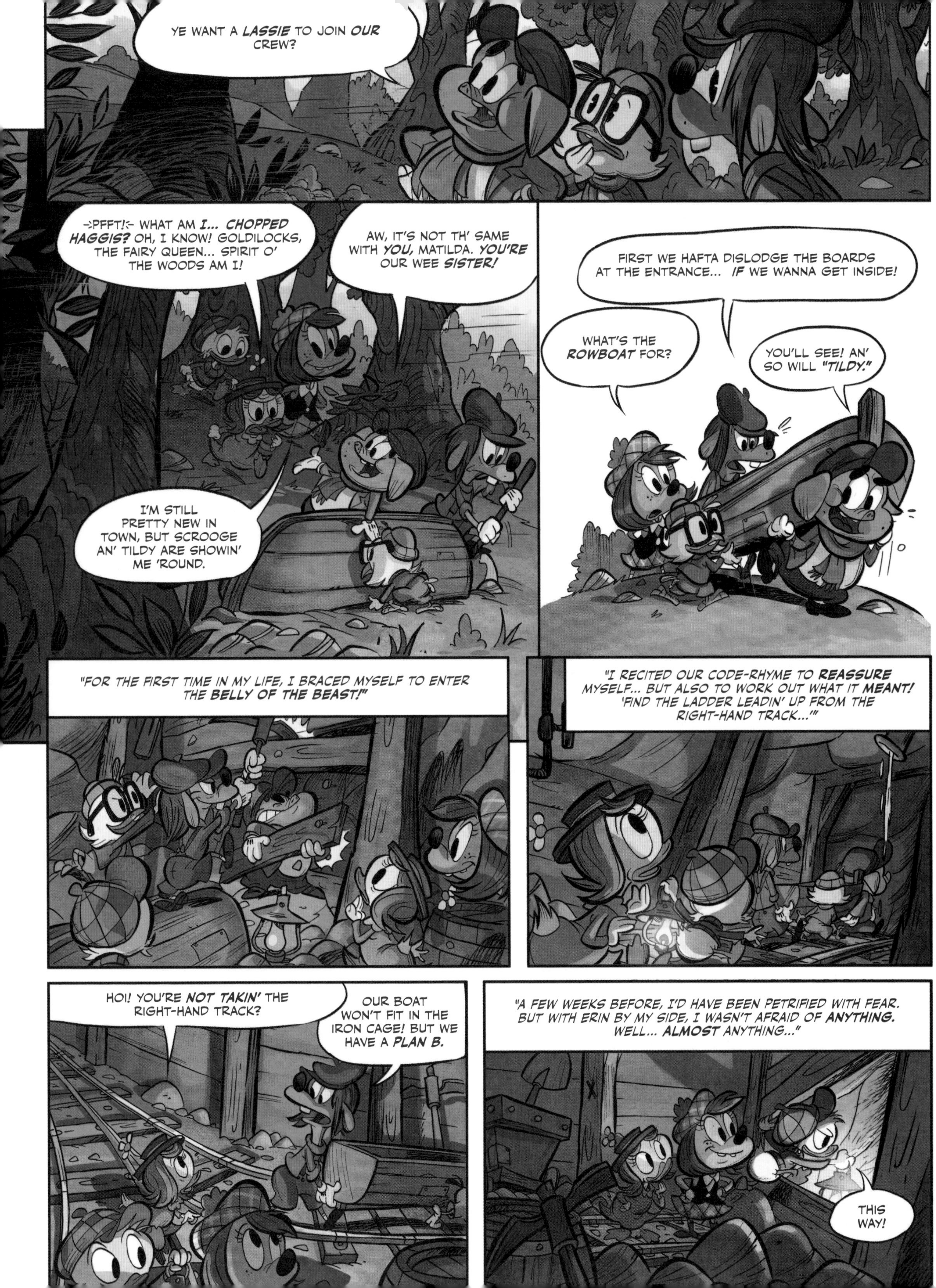
YE WANT A LASSIE TO JOIN OUR CREW?
=PFFT!= WHAT AM I... CHOPPED HAGGIS? OH, I KNOW! GOLDILOCKS, THE FAIRY QUEEN... SPIRIT O' THE WOODS AM I!
AW, IT'S NOT TH' SAME WITH YOU, MATILDA. YOU'RE OUR WEE SISTER!
I'M STILL PRETTY NEW IN TOWN, BUT SCROOGE AN' TILDY ARE SHOWIN' ME 'ROUND.
FIRST WE HAFTA DISLODGE THE BOARDS AT THE ENTRANCE... IF WE WANNA GET INSIDE!
WHAT'S THE ROWBOAT FOR?
YOU'LL SEE! AN' SO WILL "TILDY."
"FOR THE FIRST TIME IN MY LIFE, I BRACED MYSELF TO ENTER THE BELLY OF THE BEAST!"
"I RECITED OUR CODE-RHYME TO REASSURE MYSELF... BUT ALSO TO WORK OUT WHAT IT MEANT! 'FIND THE LADDER LEADIN' UP FROM THE RIGHT-HAND TRACK...'"
HOI! YOU'RE NOT TAKIN' THE RIGHT-HAND TRACK?
OUR BOAT WON'T FIT IN THE IRON CAGE! BUT WE HAVE A PLAN B.
"A FEW WEEKS BEFORE, I'D HAVE BEEN PETRIFIED WITH FEAR. BUT WITH ERIN BY MY SIDE, I WASN'T AFRAID OF ANYTHING. WELL... ALMOST ANYTHING..."
THIS WAY!

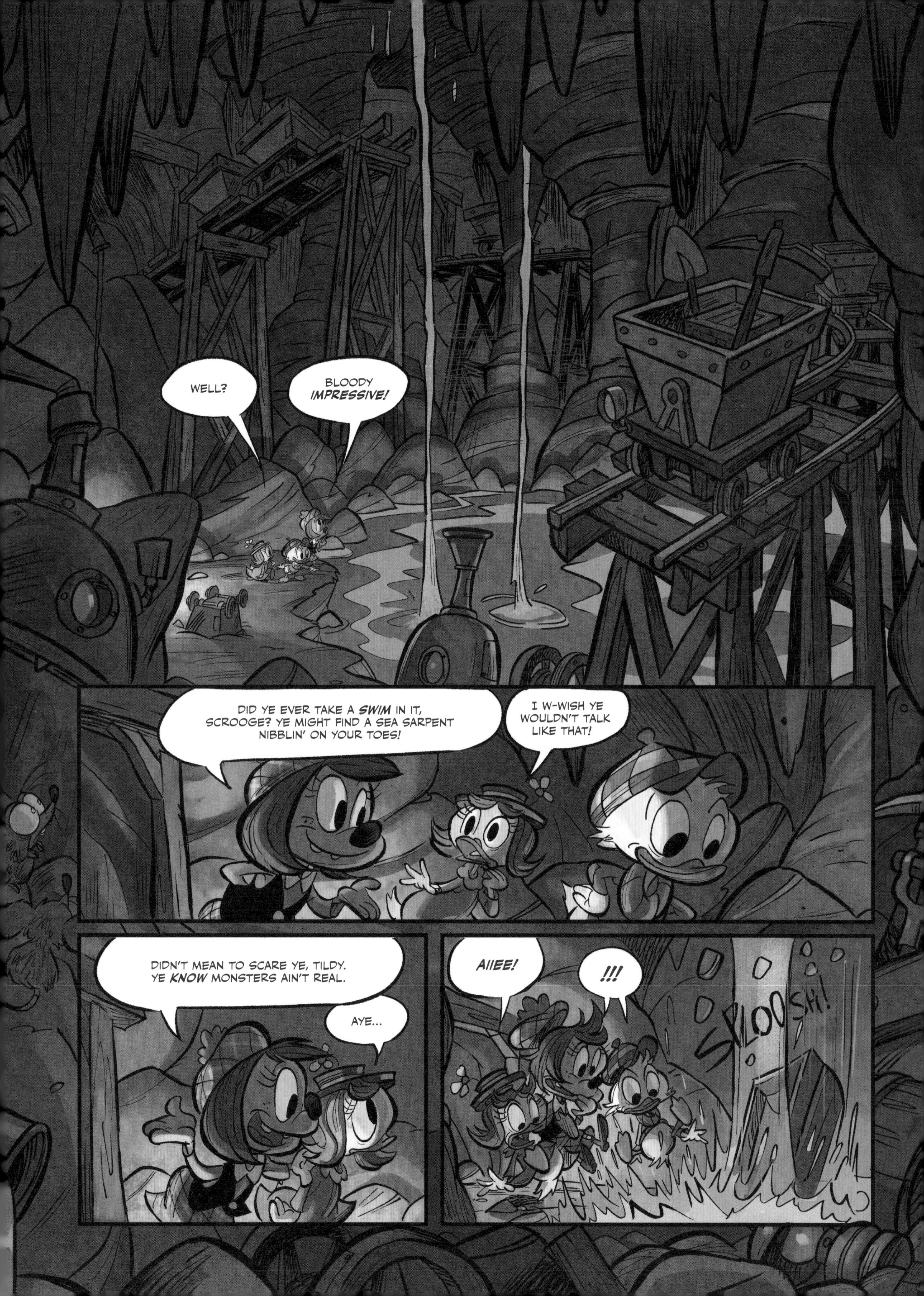
WELL?
BLOODY IMPRESSIVE!
DID YE EVER TAKE A SWIM IN IT, SCROOGE? YE MIGHT FIND A SEA SARPENT NIBBLIN' ON YOUR TOES!
I W-WISH YE WOULDN'T TALK LIKE THAT!
DIDN'T MEAN TO SCARE YE, TILDY. YE KNOW MONSTERS AIN'T REAL.
AYE...
AIIEE!
!!!
SPLOOSH!

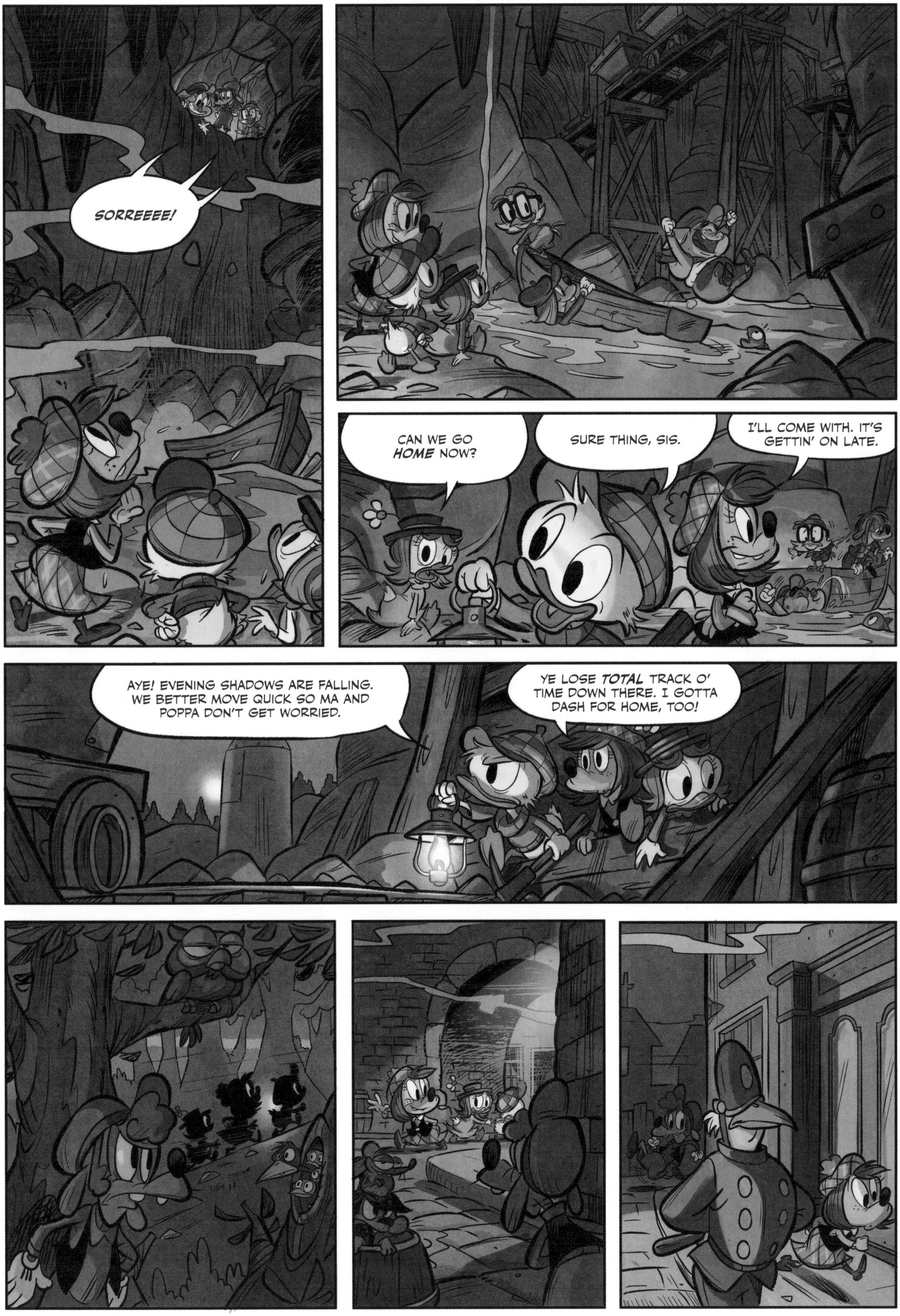
SORREEEE!
CAN WE GO HOME NOW?
SURE THING, SIS.
I'LL COME WITH. IT'S GETTIN' ON LATE.
AYE! EVENING SHADOWS ARE FALLING. WE BETTER MOVE QUICK SO MA AND POPPA DON'T GET WORRIED.
YE LOSE TOTAL TRACK O' TIME DOWN THERE. I GOTTA DASH FOR HOME, TOO!

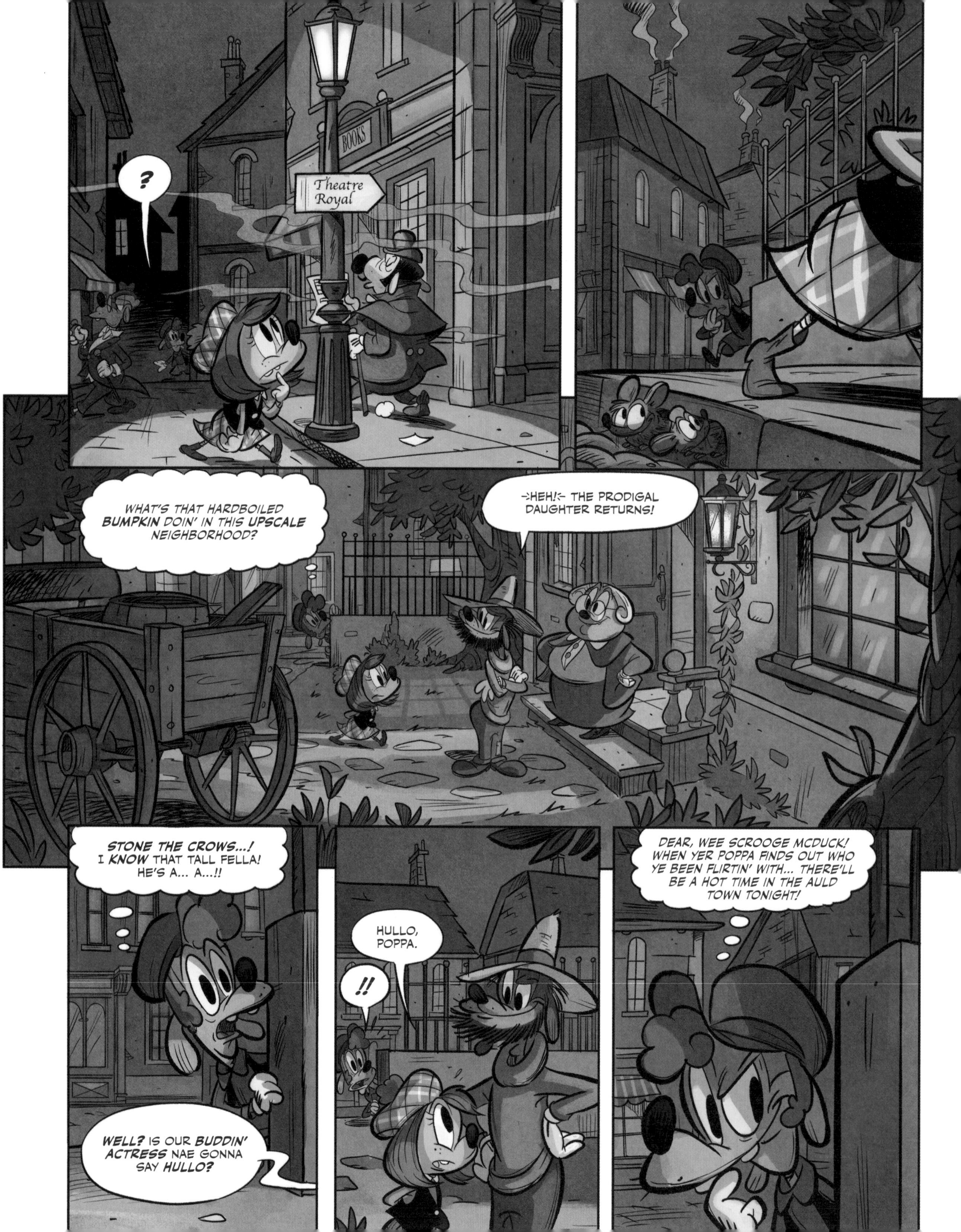

BOOKS
Theatre Royal
?
WHAT'S THAT HARDBOILED BUMPKIN DOIN' IN THIS UPSCALE NEIGHBORHOOD?
-HEH!- THE PRODIGAL DAUGHTER RETURNS!
STONE THE CROWS...! I KNOW THAT TALL FELLA! HE'S A... A...!!
WELL? IS OUR BUDDIN' ACTRESS NAE GONNA SAY HULLO?
HULLO, POPPA.
!!
DEAR, WEE SCROOGE MCDUCK! WHEN YER POPPA FINDS OUT WHO YE BEEN FLIRTIN' WITH... THERE'LL BE A HOT TIME IN THE AULD TOWN TONIGHT!

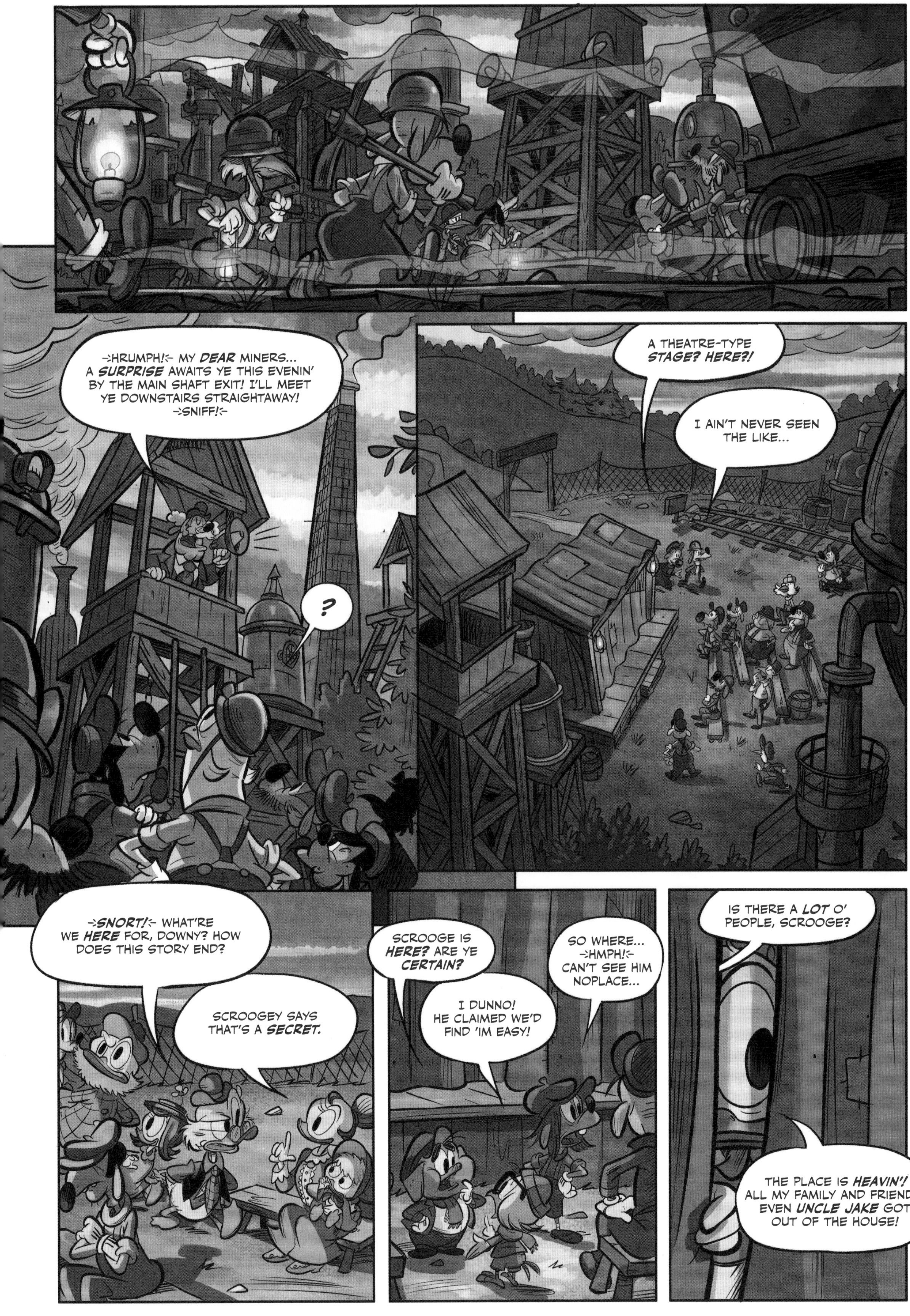
-HRUMPH!- MY DEAR MINERS... A SURPRISE AWAITS YE THIS EVENIN' BY THE MAIN SHAFT EXIT! I'LL MEET YE DOWNSTAIRS STRAIGHTAWAY! -SNIFF!-
?
A THEATRE-TYPE STAGE? HERE?!
I AIN'T NEVER SEEN THE LIKE...
-SNORT!- WHAT'RE WE HERE FOR, DOWNY? HOW DOES THIS STORY END?
SCROOGEY SAYS THAT'S A SECRET.
SCROOGE IS HERE? ARE YE CERTAIN?
I DUNNO! HE CLAIMED WE'D FIND 'IM EASY!
SO WHERE... -HMPH!- CAN'T SEE HIM NOPLACE...
IS THERE A LOT O' PEOPLE, SCROOGE?
THE PLACE IS HEAVIN'! ALL MY FAMILY AND FRIENDS. EVEN UNCLE JAKE GOT OUT OF THE HOUSE!

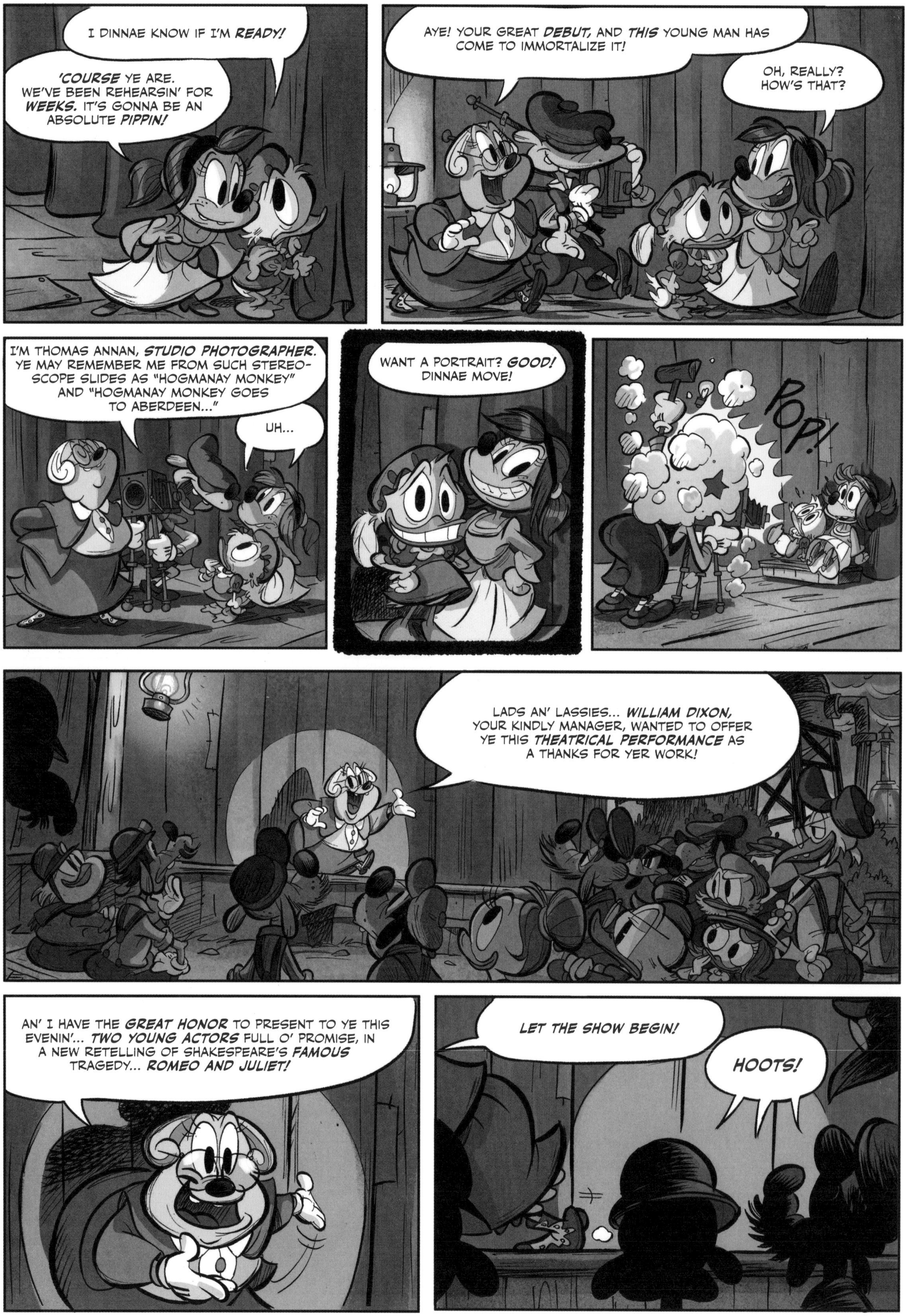
I DINNAE KNOW IF I'M READY!
'COURSE YE ARE. WE'VE BEEN REHEARSIN' FOR WEEKS. IT'S GONNA BE AN ABSOLUTE PIPPIN!
AYE! YOUR GREAT DEBUT, AND THIS YOUNG MAN HAS COME TO IMMORTALIZE IT!
OH, REALLY? HOW'S THAT?
I'M THOMAS ANNAN, STUDIO PHOTOGRAPHER. YE MAY REMEMBER ME FROM SUCH STEREO-SCOPE SLIDES AS "HOGMANAY MONKEY" AND "HOGMANAY MONKEY GOES TO ABERDEEN..."
UH...
WANT A PORTRAIT? GOOD! DINNAE MOVE!
POP!
LADS AN' LASSIES... WILLIAM DIXON, YOUR KINDLY MANAGER, WANTED TO OFFER YE THIS THEATRICAL PERFORMANCE AS A THANKS FOR YER WORK!
AN' I HAVE THE GREAT HONOR TO PRESENT TO YE THIS EVENIN'... TWO YOUNG ACTORS FULL O' PROMISE, IN A NEW RETELLING OF SHAKESPEARE'S FAMOUS TRAGEDY... ROMEO AND JULIET!
LET THE SHOW BEGIN!
HOOTS!

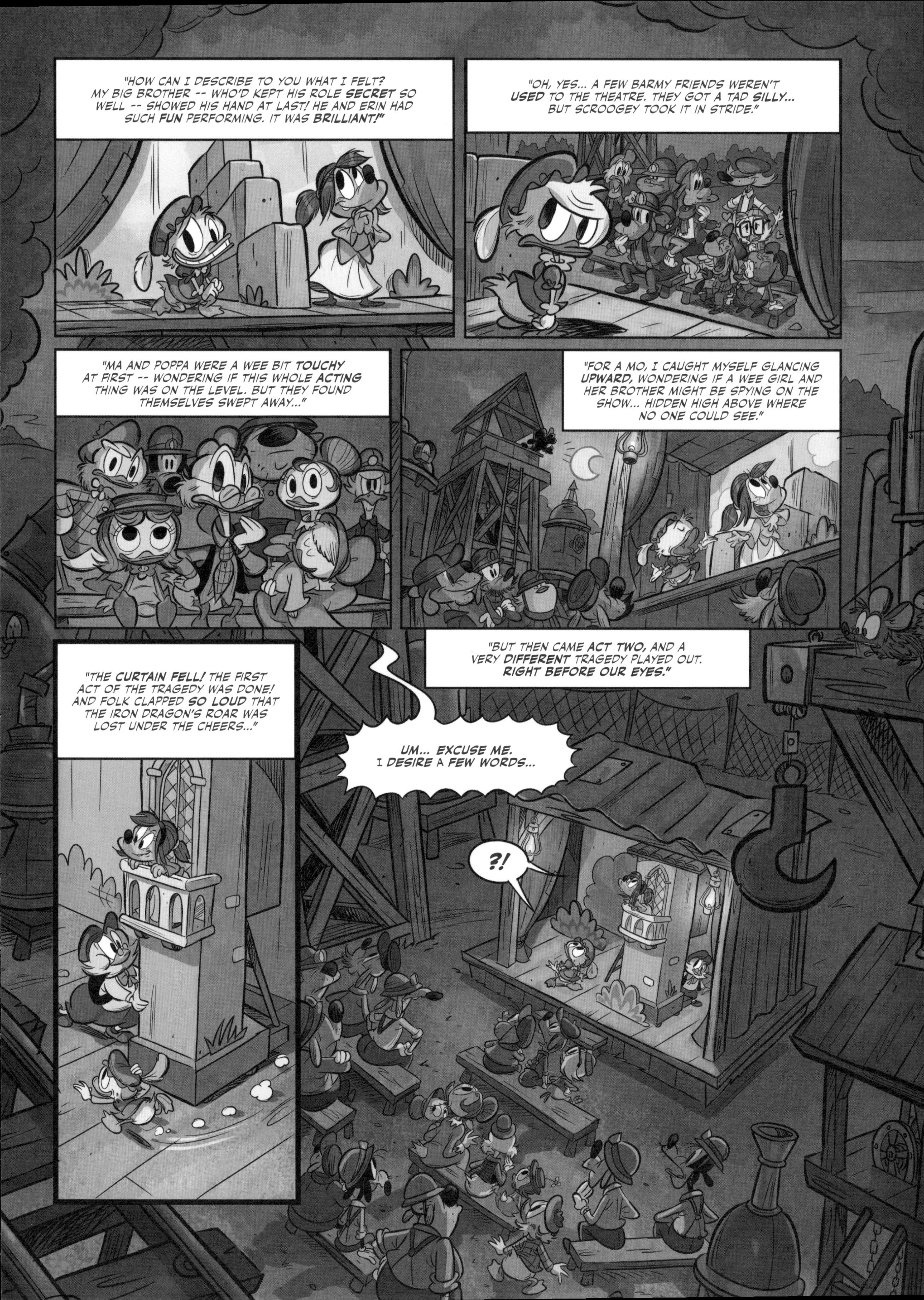
"HOW CAN I DESCRIBE TO YOU WHAT I FELT? MY BIG BROTHER -- WHO'D KEPT HIS ROLE SECRET SO WELL -- SHOWED HIS HAND AT LAST! HE AND ERIN HAD SUCH FUN PERFORMING. IT WAS BRILLIANT!"
"OH, YES... A FEW BARMY FRIENDS WEREN'T USED TO THE THEATRE. THEY GOT A TAD SILLY... BUT SCROOGEY TOOK IT IN STRIDE."
"MA AND POPPA WERE A WEE BIT TOUCHY AT FIRST -- WONDERING IF THIS WHOLE ACTING THING WAS ON THE LEVEL. BUT THEY FOUND THEMSELVES SWEPT AWAY..."
"FOR A MO, I CAUGHT MYSELF GLANCING UPWARD, WONDERING IF A WEE GIRL AND HER BROTHER MIGHT BE SPYING ON THE SHOW... HIDDEN HIGH ABOVE WHERE NO ONE COULD SEE."
"THE CURTAIN FELL! THE FIRST ACT OF THE TRAGEDY WAS DONE! AND FOLK CLAPPED SO LOUD THAT THE IRON DRAGON'S ROAR WAS LOST UNDER THE CHEERS..."
"BUT THEN CAME ACT TWO, AND A VERY DIFFERENT TRAGEDY PLAYED OUT. RIGHT BEFORE OUR EYES."
UM... EXCUSE ME. I DESIRE A FEW WORDS...
?!

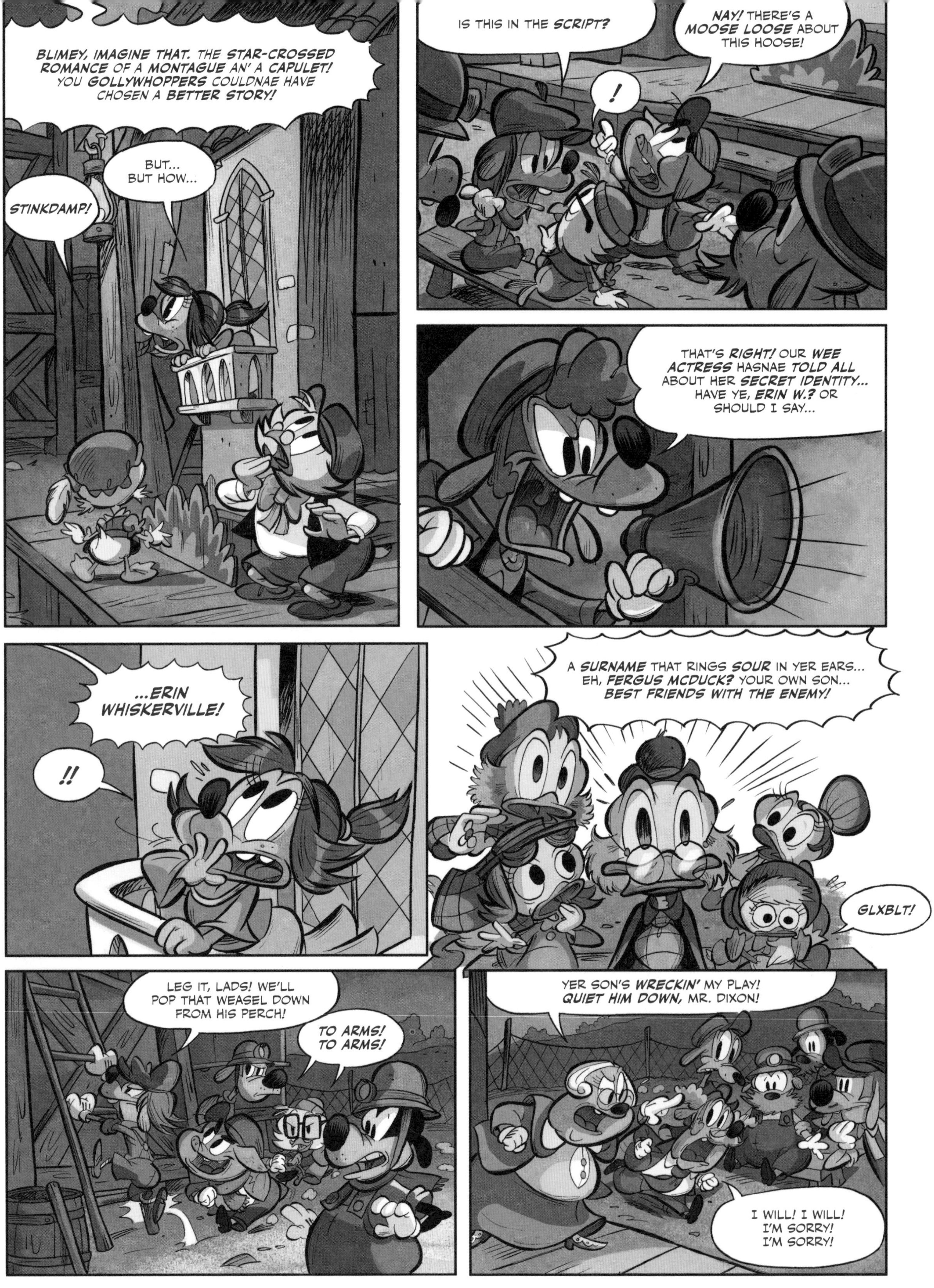

BLIMEY, IMAGINE THAT. THE STAR-CROSSED ROMANCE OF A MONTAGUE AN' A CAPULET! YOU GOLLYWHOPPERS COULDNAE HAVE CHOSEN A BETTER STORY!
BUT... BUT HOW...
STINKDAMP!
IS THIS IN THE SCRIPT?
NAY! THERE'S A MOOSE LOOSE ABOUT THIS HOOSE!
!
THAT'S RIGHT! OUR WEE ACTRESS HASNAE TOLD ALL ABOUT HER SECRET IDENTITY... HAVE YE, ERIN W.? OR SHOULD I SAY...
...ERIN WHISKERVILLE!
!!
A SURNAME THAT RINGS SOUR IN YER EARS... EH, FERGUS MCDUCK? YOUR OWN SON... BEST FRIENDS WITH THE ENEMY!
GLXBLT!
LEG IT, LADS! WE'LL POP THAT WEASEL DOWN FROM HIS PERCH!
TO ARMS! TO ARMS!
YER SON'S WRECKIN' MY PLAY! QUIET HIM DOWN, MR. DIXON!
I WILL! I WILL! I'M SORRY! I'M SORRY!

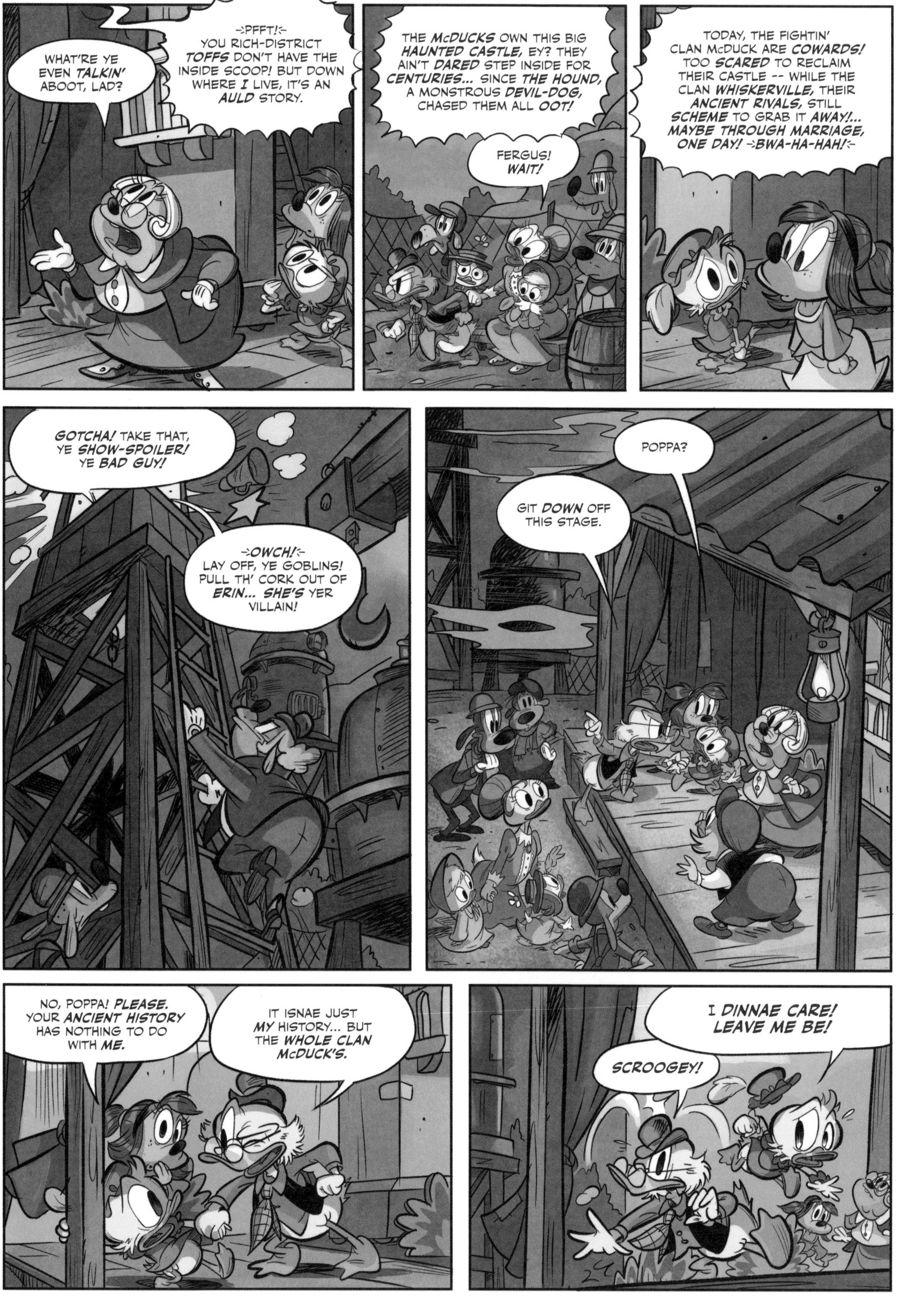
WHAT'RE YE EVEN TALKIN' ABOOT, LAD?
-PFFT!- YOU RICH-DISTRICT TOFFS DON'T HAVE THE INSIDE SCOOP! BUT DOWN WHERE I LIVE, IT'S AN AULD STORY.
THE McDUCKS OWN THIS BIG HAUNTED CASTLE, EY? THEY AIN'T DARED STEP INSIDE FOR CENTURIES... SINCE THE HOUND, A MONSTROUS DEVIL-DOG, CHASED THEM ALL OOT!
FERGUS! WAIT!
TODAY, THE FIGHTIN' CLAN McDUCK ARE COWARDS! TOO SCARED TO RECLAIM THEIR CASTLE -- WHILE THE CLAN WHISKERVILLE, THEIR ANCIENT RIVALS, STILL SCHEME TO GRAB IT AWAY!... MAYBE THROUGH MARRIAGE, ONE DAY! -BWA-HA-HAH!-
GOTCHA! TAKE THAT, YE SHOW-SPOILER! YE BAD GUY!
-OWCH!- LAY OFF, YE GOBLINS! PULL TH' CORK OUT OF ERIN... SHE'S YER VILLAIN!
POPPA?
GIT DOWN OFF THIS STAGE.
NO, POPPA! PLEASE. YOUR ANCIENT HISTORY HAS NOTHING TO DO WITH ME.
IT ISNAE JUST MY HISTORY... BUT THE WHOLE CLAN McDUCK'S.
I DINNAE CARE! LEAVE ME BE!
SCROOGEY!

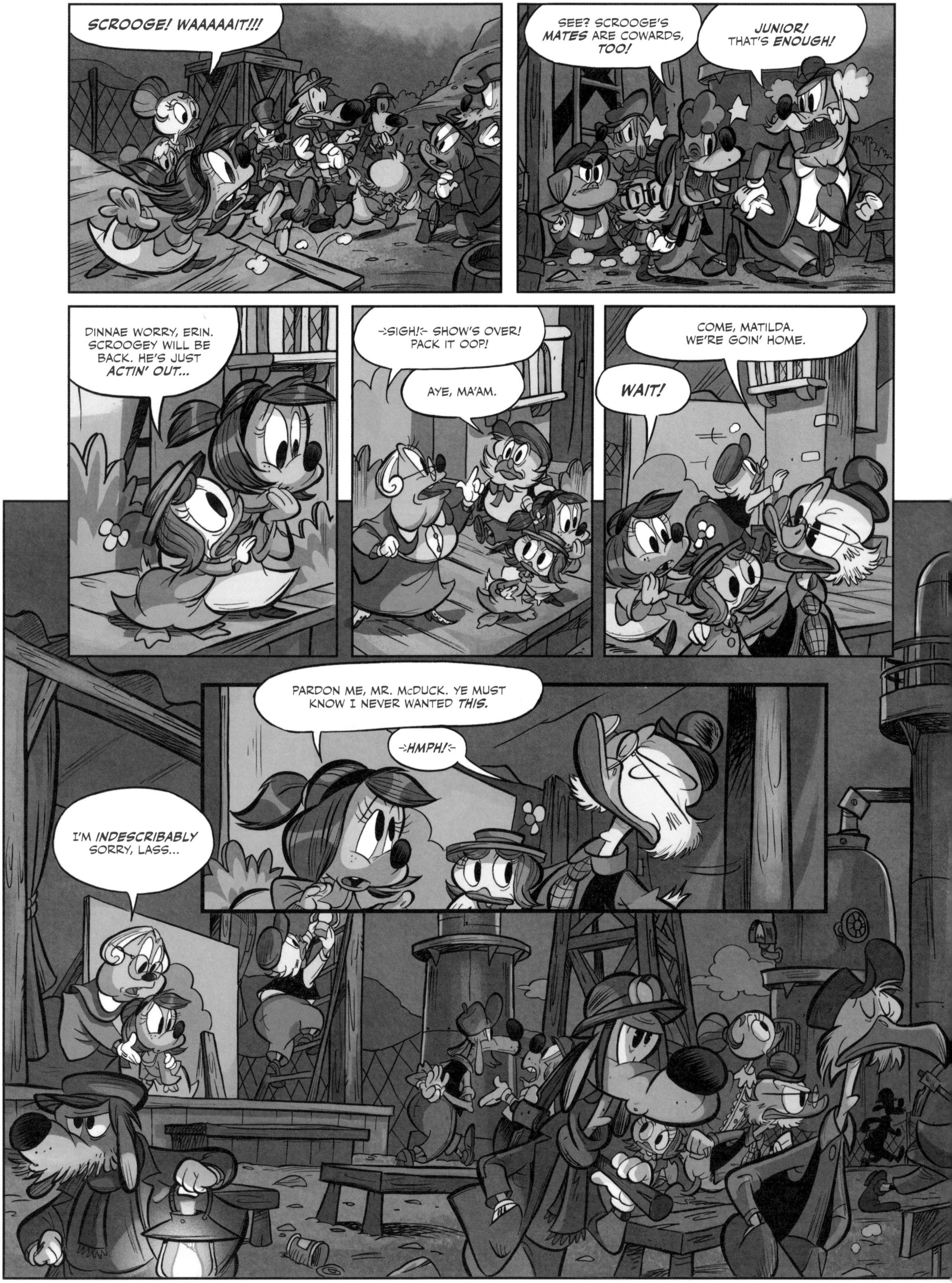
SCROOGE! WAAAAAIT!!!
SEE? SCROOGE'S MATES ARE COWARDS, TOO!
JUNIOR! THAT'S ENOUGH!
DINNAE WORRY, ERIN. SCROOGEY WILL BE BACK. HE'S JUST ACTIN' OUT...
-SIGH!- SHOW'S OVER! PACK IT OOP!
AYE, MA'AM.
COME, MATILDA. WE'RE GOIN' HOME.
WAIT!
PARDON ME, MR. McDUCK. YE MUST KNOW I NEVER WANTED THIS.
-HMPH!-
I'M INDESCRIBABLY SORRY, LASS...

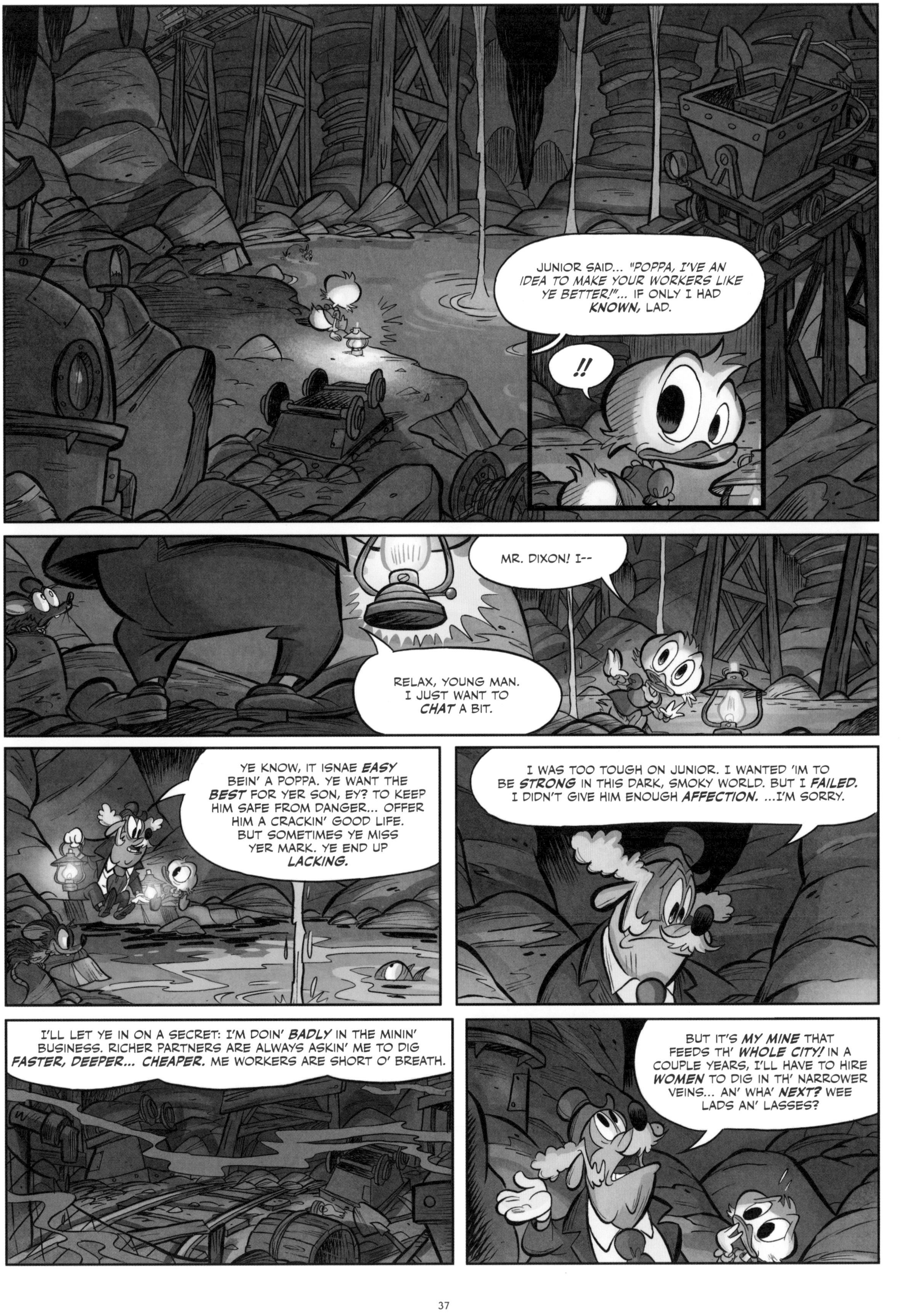

JUNIOR SAID... "POPPA, I'VE AN IDEA TO MAKE YOUR WORKERS LIKE YE BETTER!"... IF ONLY I HAD KNOWN, LAD.
!!
MR. DIXON! I--
RELAX, YOUNG MAN. I JUST WANT TO CHAT A BIT.
YE KNOW, IT ISNAE EASY BEIN' A POPPA. YE WANT THE BEST FOR YER SON, EY? TO KEEP HIM SAFE FROM DANGER... OFFER HIM A CRACKIN' GOOD LIFE. BUT SOMETIMES YE MISS YER MARK. YE END UP LACKING.
I WAS TOO TOUGH ON JUNIOR. I WANTED 'IM TO BE STRONG IN THIS DARK, SMOKY WORLD. BUT I FAILED. I DIDN'T GIVE HIM ENOUGH AFFECTION. ...I'M SORRY.
I'LL LET YE IN ON A SECRET: I'M DOIN' BADLY IN THE MININ' BUSINESS. RICHER PARTNERS ARE ALWAYS ASKIN' ME TO DIG FASTER, DEEPER... CHEAPER. ME WORKERS ARE SHORT O' BREATH.
BUT IT'S MY MINE THAT FEEDS TH' WHOLE CITY! IN A COUPLE YEARS, I'LL HAVE TO HIRE WOMEN TO DIG IN TH' NARROWER VEINS... AN' WHA' NEXT? WEE LADS AN' LASSES?

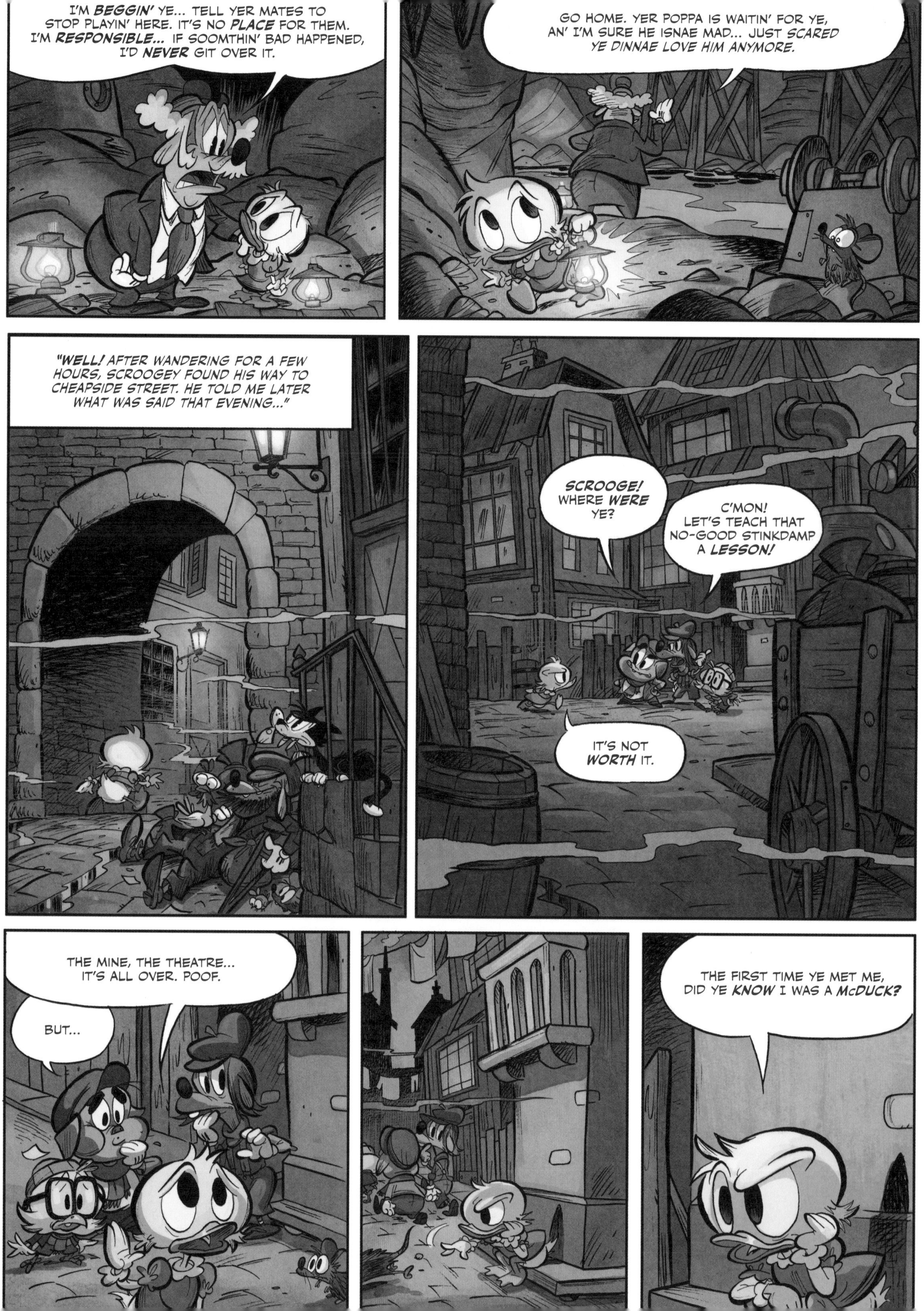
I'M BEGGIN' YE... TELL YER MATES TO STOP PLAYIN' HERE. IT'S NO PLACE FOR THEM. I'M RESPONSIBLE... IF SOOMTHIN' BAD HAPPENED, I'D NEVER GIT OVER IT.
GO HOME. YER POPPA IS WAITIN' FOR YE, AN' I'M SURE HE ISNAE MAD... JUST SCARED YE DINNAE LOVE HIM ANYMORE.
"WELL! AFTER WANDERING FOR A FEW HOURS, SCROOGEY FOUND HIS WAY TO CHEAPSIDE STREET. HE TOLD ME LATER WHAT WAS SAID THAT EVENING..."
SCROOGE! WHERE WERE YE?
C'MON! LET'S TEACH THAT NO-GOOD STINKDAMP A LESSON!
IT'S NOT WORTH IT.
THE MINE, THE THEATRE... IT'S ALL OVER. POOF.
BUT...
THE FIRST TIME YE MET ME, DID YE KNOW I WAS A McDUCK?

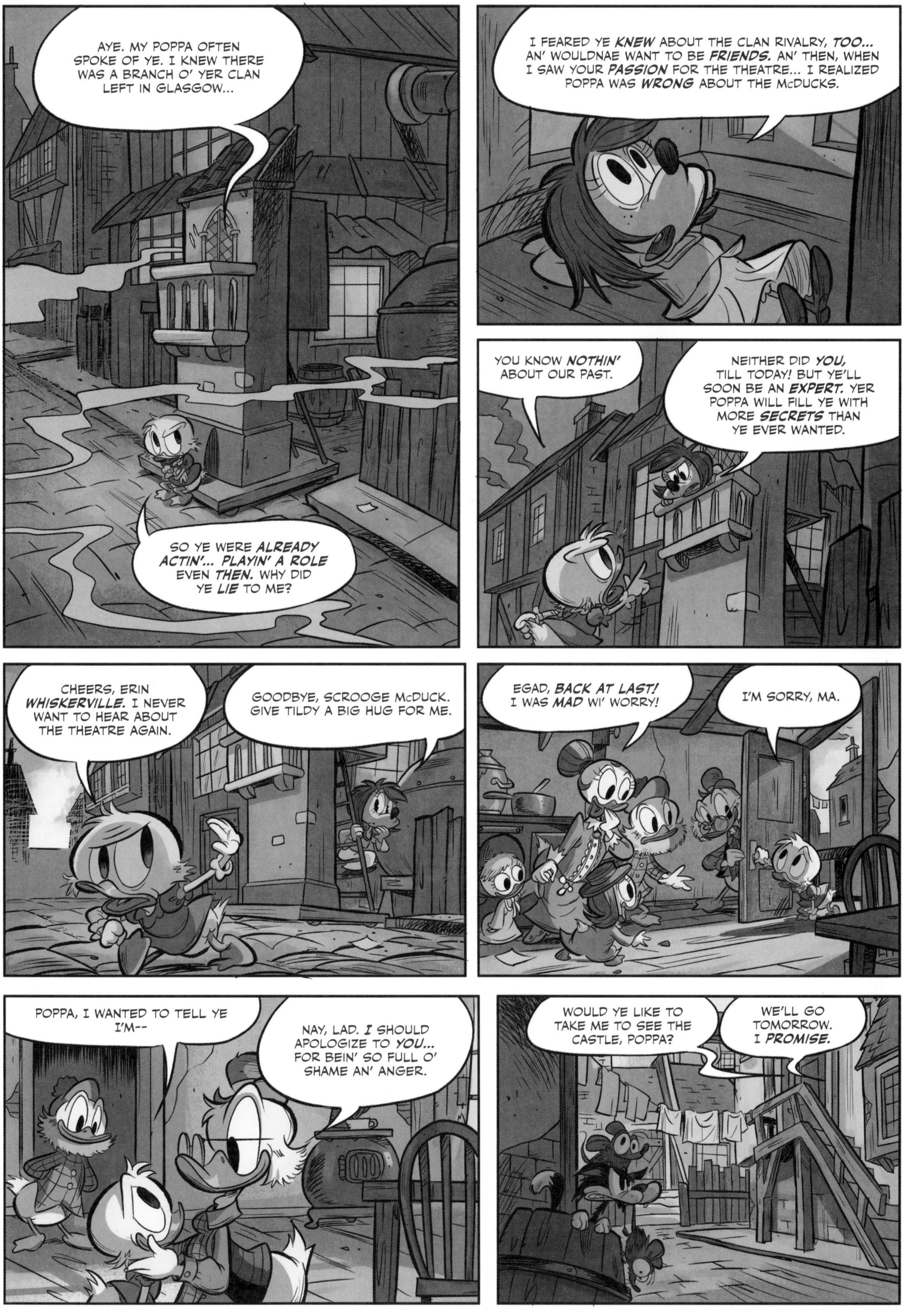
AYE. MY POPPA OFTEN SPOKE OF YE. I KNEW THERE WAS A BRANCH O' YER CLAN LEFT IN GLASGOW...
SO YE WERE ALREADY ACTIN'... PLAYIN' A ROLE EVEN THEN. WHY DID YE LIE TO ME?
I FEARED YE KNEW ABOUT THE CLAN RIVALRY, TOO... AN' WOULDNAE WANT TO BE FRIENDS. AN' THEN, WHEN I SAW YOUR PASSION FOR THE THEATRE... I REALIZED POPPA WAS WRONG ABOUT THE McDUCKS.
YOU KNOW NOTHIN' ABOUT OUR PAST.
NEITHER DID YOU, TILL TODAY! BUT YE'LL SOON BE AN EXPERT. YER POPPA WILL FILL YE WITH MORE SECRETS THAN YE EVER WANTED.
CHEERS, ERIN WHISKERVILLE. I NEVER WANT TO HEAR ABOUT THE THEATRE AGAIN.
GOODBYE, SCROOGE McDUCK. GIVE TILDY A BIG HUG FOR ME.
EGAD, BACK AT LAST! I WAS MAD WI' WORRY!
I'M SORRY, MA.
POPPA, I WANTED TO TELL YE I'M--
NAY, LAD. I SHOULD APOLOGIZE TO YOU... FOR BEIN' SO FULL O' SHAME AN' ANGER.
WOULD YE LIKE TO TAKE ME TO SEE THE CASTLE, POPPA?
WE'LL GO TOMORROW. I PROMISE.

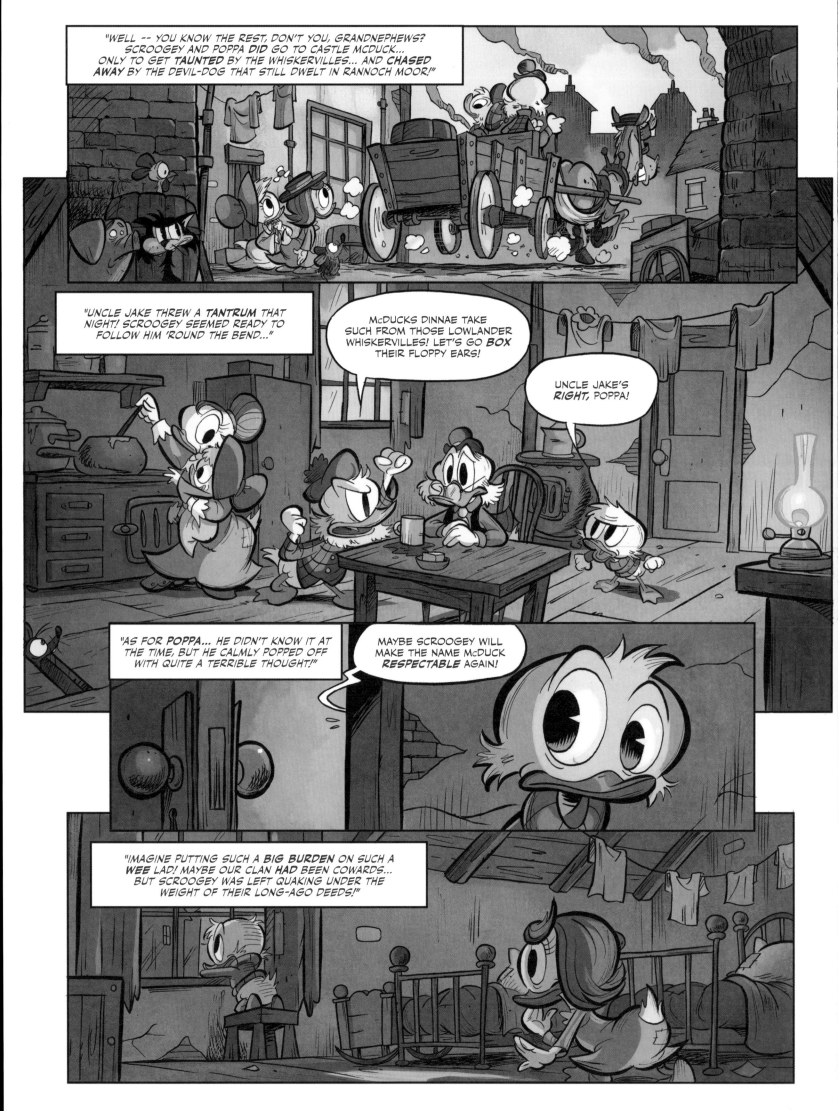

"WELL -- YOU KNOW THE REST, DON'T YOU, GRANDNEPHEWS? SCROOGEY AND POPPA *DID* GO TO CASTLE MCDUCK... ONLY TO GET *TAUNTED* BY THE WHISKERVILLES... AND *CHASED AWAY* BY THE DEVIL-DOG THAT STILL DWELT IN RANNOCH MOOR!"

"UNCLE JAKE THREW A *TANTRUM* THAT NIGHT! SCROOGEY SEEMED READY TO FOLLOW HIM 'ROUND THE BEND..."

McDUCKS DINNAE TAKE SUCH FROM THOSE LOWLANDER WHISKERVILLES! LET'S GO *BOX* THEIR FLOPPY EARS!

UNCLE JAKE'S *RIGHT*, POPPA!

"AS FOR *POPPA*... HE DIDN'T KNOW IT AT THE TIME, BUT HE CALMLY POPPED OFF WITH QUITE A TERRIBLE THOUGHT!"

MAYBE SCROOGEY WILL MAKE THE NAME McDUCK *RESPECTABLE* AGAIN!

"IMAGINE PUTTING SUCH A *BIG BURDEN* ON SUCH A *WEE* LAD! MAYBE OUR CLAN *HAD* BEEN COWARDS... BUT SCROOGEY WAS LEFT QUAKING UNDER THE WEIGHT OF THEIR LONG-AGO DEEDS!"

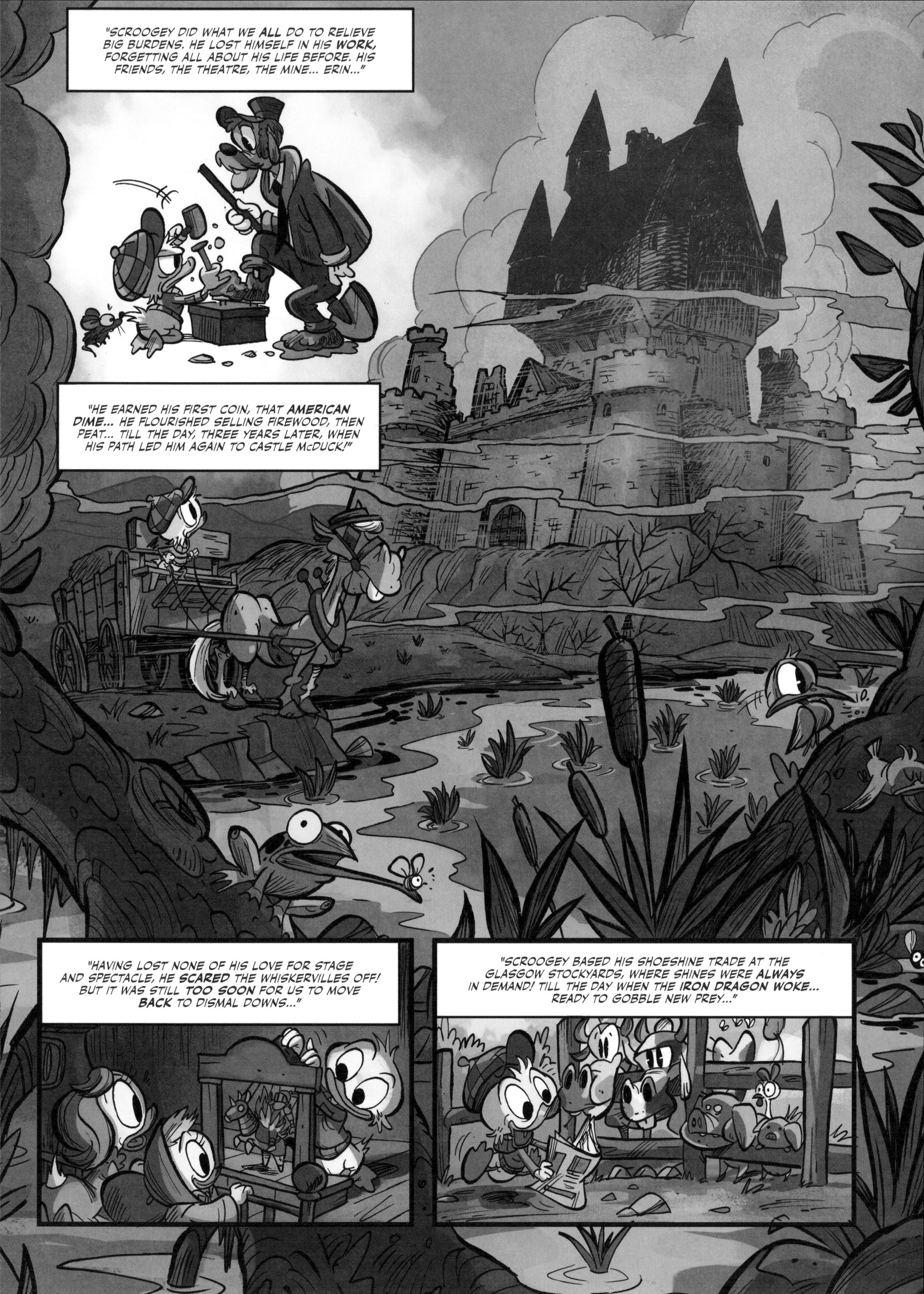
"SCROOGEY DID WHAT WE ALL DO TO RELIEVE BIG BURDENS. HE LOST HIMSELF IN HIS WORK, FORGETTING ALL ABOUT HIS LIFE BEFORE. HIS FRIENDS, THE THEATRE, THE MINE... ERIN..."
"HE EARNED HIS FIRST COIN, THAT AMERICAN DIME... HE FLOURISHED SELLING FIREWOOD, THEN PEAT... TILL THE DAY, THREE YEARS LATER, WHEN HIS PATH LED HIM AGAIN TO CASTLE McDUCK!"
"HAVING LOST NONE OF HIS LOVE FOR STAGE AND SPECTACLE, HE SCARED THE WHISKERVILLES OFF! BUT IT WAS STILL TOO SOON FOR US TO MOVE BACK TO DISMAL DOWNS..."
"SCROOGEY BASED HIS SHOESHINE TRADE AT THE GLASGOW STOCKYARDS, WHERE SHINES WERE ALWAYS IN DEMAND! TILL THE DAY WHEN THE IRON DRAGON WOKE... READY TO GOBBLE NEW PREY..."

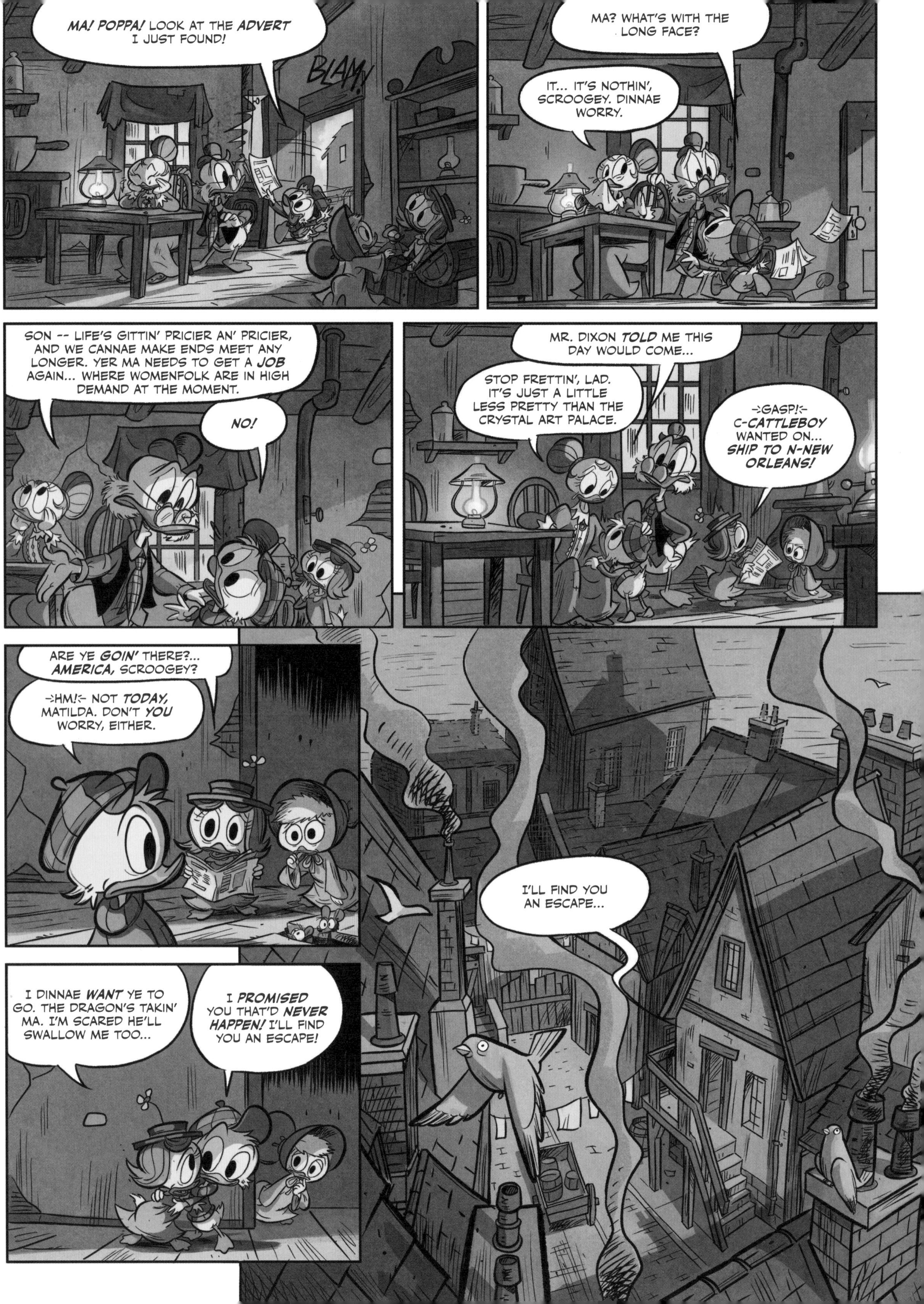

MA! POPPA! LOOK AT THE ADVERT I JUST FOUND!
BLAM!
MA? WHAT'S WITH THE LONG FACE?
IT... IT'S NOTHIN', SCROOGEY. DINNAE WORRY.
SON -- LIFE'S GITTIN' PRICIER AN' PRICIER, AND WE CANNAE MAKE ENDS MEET ANY LONGER. YER MA NEEDS TO GET A JOB AGAIN... WHERE WOMENFOLK ARE IN HIGH DEMAND AT THE MOMENT.
NO!
MR. DIXON TOLD ME THIS DAY WOULD COME...
STOP FRETTIN', LAD. IT'S JUST A LITTLE LESS PRETTY THAN THE CRYSTAL ART PALACE.
-GASP!- C-CATTLEBOY WANTED ON... SHIP TO N-NEW ORLEANS!
ARE YE GOIN' THERE?... AMERICA, SCROOGEY?
-HM!- NOT TODAY, MATILDA. DON'T YOU WORRY, EITHER.
I'LL FIND YOU AN ESCAPE...
I DINNAE WANT YE TO GO. THE DRAGON'S TAKIN' MA. I'M SCARED HE'LL SWALLOW ME TOO...
I PROMISED YOU THAT'D NEVER HAPPEN! I'LL FIND YOU AN ESCAPE!

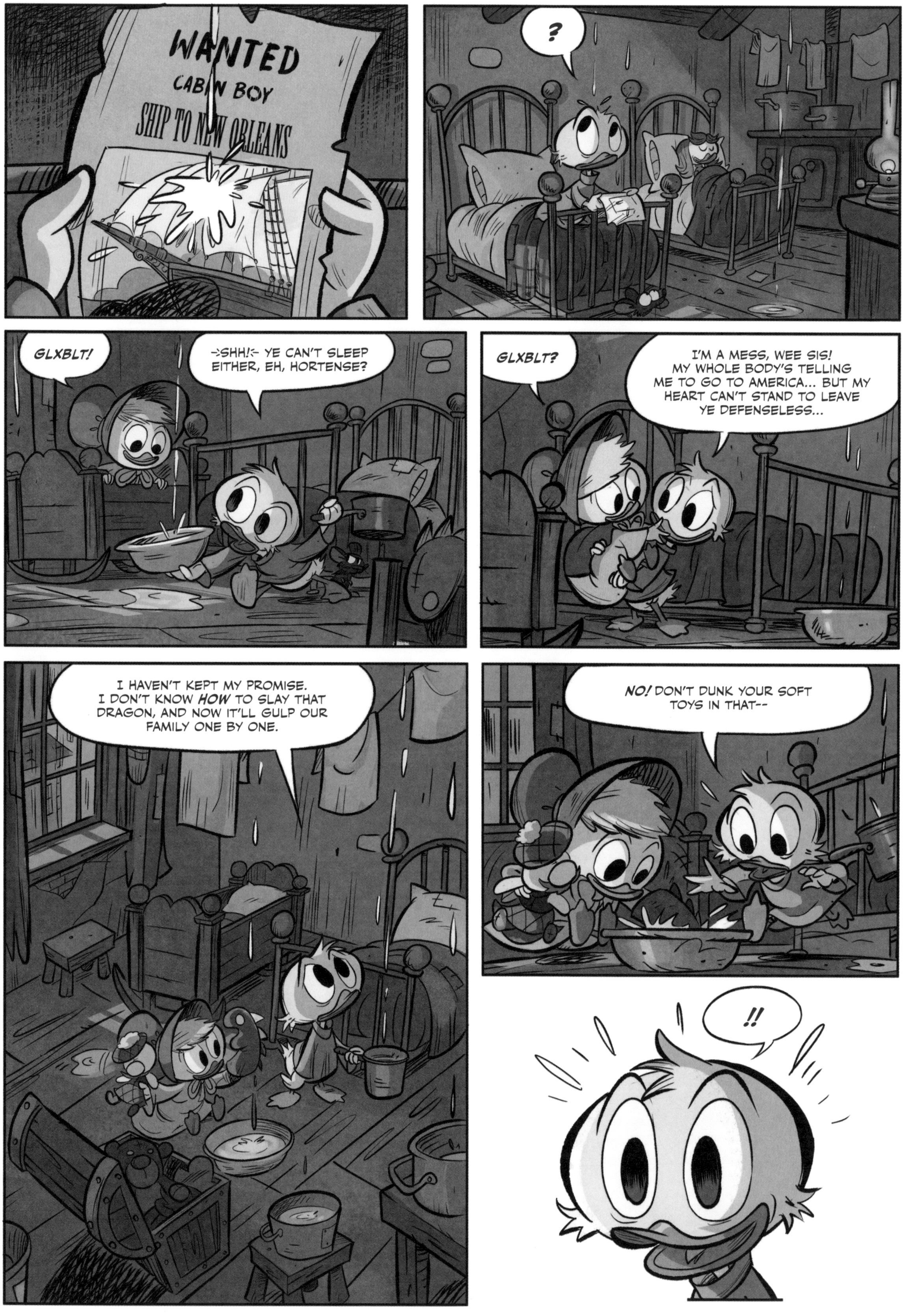

WANTED
CABIN BOY
SHIP TO NEW ORLEANS
?
GLXBLT!
-SHH!- YE CAN'T SLEEP EITHER, EH, HORTENSE?
GLXBLT?
I'M A MESS, WEE SIS! MY WHOLE BODY'S TELLING ME TO GO TO AMERICA... BUT MY HEART CAN'T STAND TO LEAVE YE DEFENSELESS...
I HAVEN'T KEPT MY PROMISE. I DON'T KNOW *HOW* TO SLAY THAT DRAGON, AND NOW IT'LL GULP OUR FAMILY ONE BY ONE.
NO! DON'T DUNK YOUR SOFT TOYS IN THAT--
!!

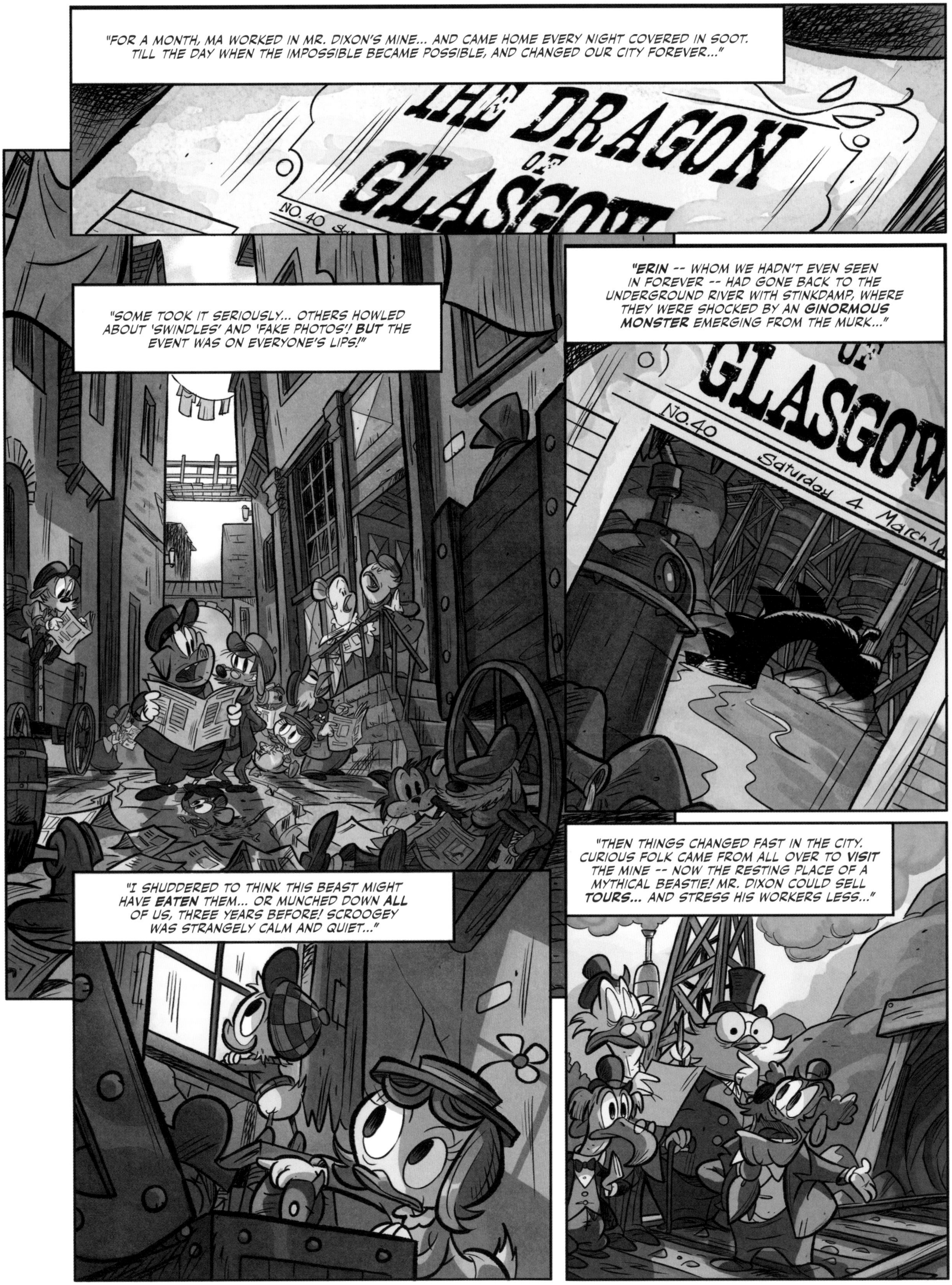
"FOR A MONTH, MA WORKED IN MR. DIXON'S MINE... AND CAME HOME EVERY NIGHT COVERED IN SOOT. TILL THE DAY WHEN THE IMPOSSIBLE BECAME POSSIBLE, AND CHANGED OUR CITY FOREVER..."
THE DRAGON OF GLASGOW
NO. 40
"SOME TOOK IT SERIOUSLY... OTHERS HOWLED ABOUT 'SWINDLES' AND 'FAKE PHOTOS'! BUT THE EVENT WAS ON EVERYONE'S LIPS!"
"ERIN -- WHOM WE HADN'T EVEN SEEN IN FOREVER -- HAD GONE BACK TO THE UNDERGROUND RIVER WITH STINKDAMP, WHERE THEY WERE SHOCKED BY AN GINORMOUS MONSTER EMERGING FROM THE MURK..."
GLASGOW
No. 40 Saturday 4 March
"I SHUDDERED TO THINK THIS BEAST MIGHT HAVE EATEN THEM... OR MUNCHED DOWN ALL OF US, THREE YEARS BEFORE! SCROOGEY WAS STRANGELY CALM AND QUIET..."
"THEN THINGS CHANGED FAST IN THE CITY. CURIOUS FOLK CAME FROM ALL OVER TO VISIT THE MINE -- NOW THE RESTING PLACE OF A MYTHICAL BEASTIE! MR. DIXON COULD SELL TOURS... AND STRESS HIS WORKERS LESS..."

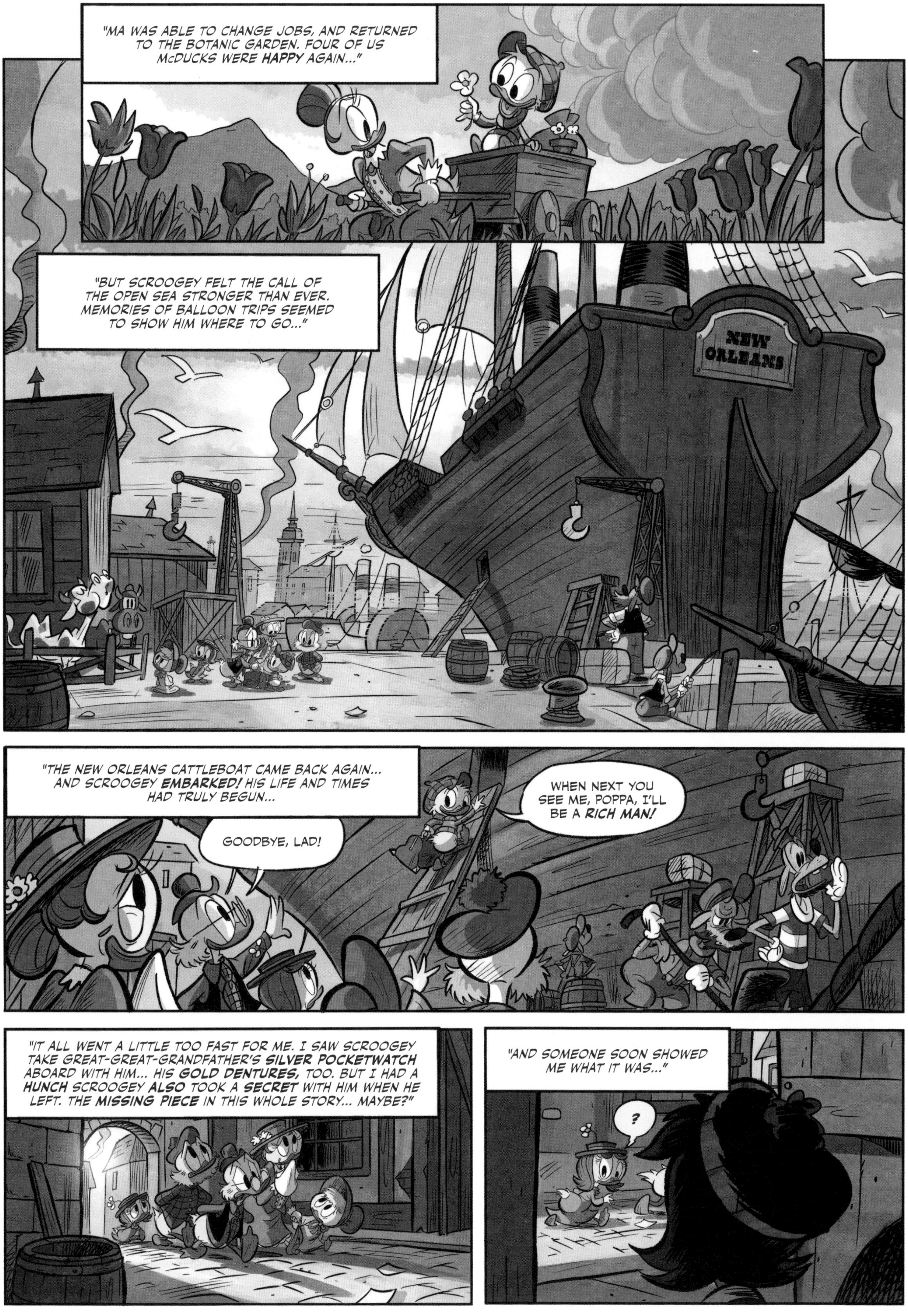
"MA WAS ABLE TO CHANGE JOBS, AND RETURNED TO THE BOTANIC GARDEN. FOUR OF US McDUCKS WERE HAPPY AGAIN..."
"BUT SCROOGEY FELT THE CALL OF THE OPEN SEA STRONGER THAN EVER. MEMORIES OF BALLOON TRIPS SEEMED TO SHOW HIM WHERE TO GO..."
NEW ORLEANS
"THE NEW ORLEANS CATTLEBOAT CAME BACK AGAIN... AND SCROOGEY EMBARKED! HIS LIFE AND TIMES HAD TRULY BEGUN...
WHEN NEXT YOU SEE ME, POPPA, I'LL BE A RICH MAN!
GOODBYE, LAD!
"IT ALL WENT A LITTLE TOO FAST FOR ME. I SAW SCROOGEY TAKE GREAT-GREAT-GRANDFATHER'S SILVER POCKETWATCH ABOARD WITH HIM... HIS GOLD DENTURES, TOO. BUT I HAD A HUNCH SCROOGEY ALSO TOOK A SECRET WITH HIM WHEN HE LEFT. THE MISSING PIECE IN THIS WHOLE STORY... MAYBE?"
"AND SOMEONE SOON SHOWED ME WHAT IT WAS..."
?

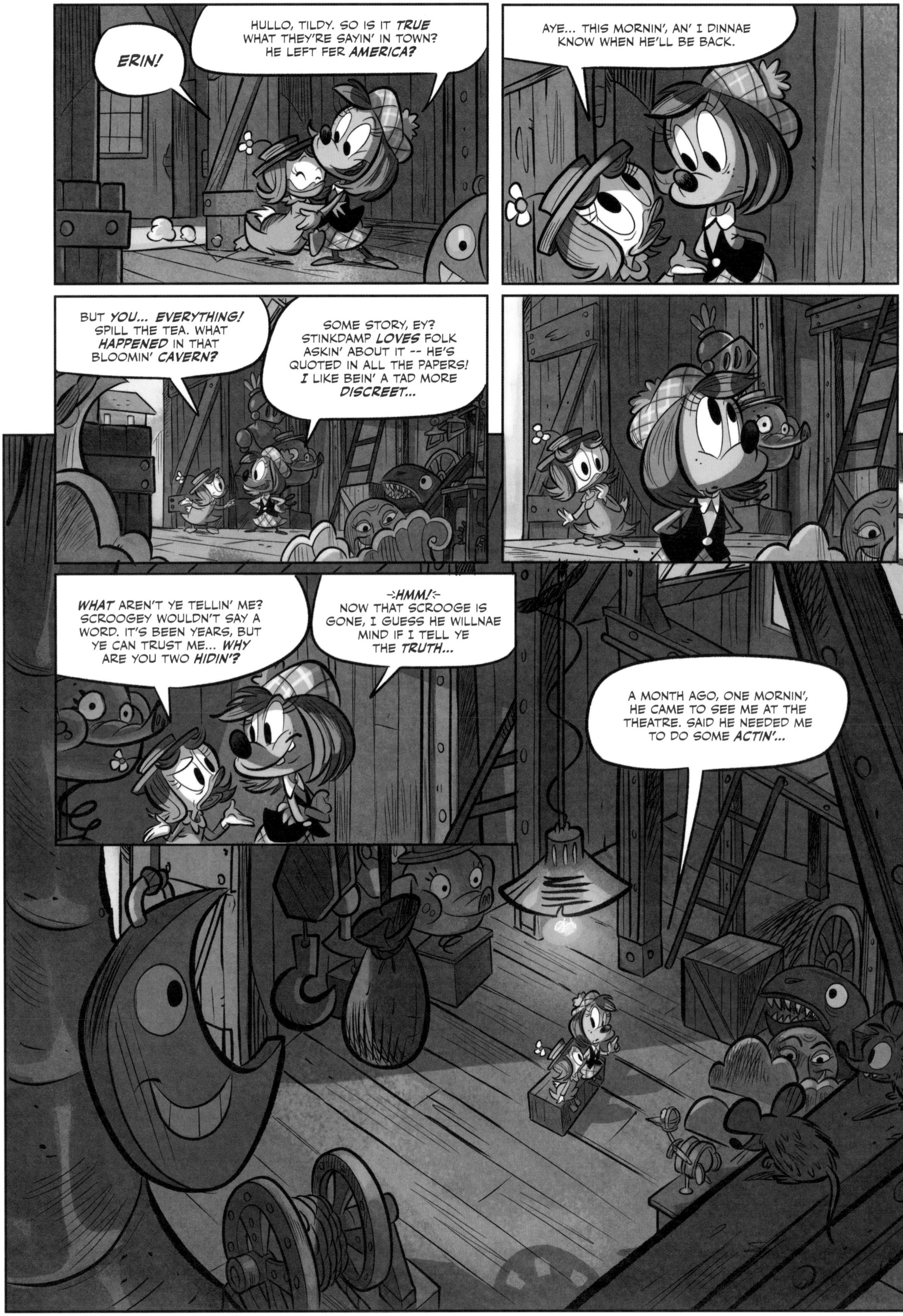

ERIN!
HULLO, TILDY. SO IS IT TRUE WHAT THEY'RE SAYIN' IN TOWN? HE LEFT FER AMERICA?
AYE... THIS MORNIN', AN' I DINNAE KNOW WHEN HE'LL BE BACK.
BUT YOU... EVERYTHING! SPILL THE TEA. WHAT HAPPENED IN THAT BLOOMIN' CAVERN?
SOME STORY, EY? STINKDAMP LOVES FOLK ASKIN' ABOUT IT -- HE'S QUOTED IN ALL THE PAPERS! I LIKE BEIN' A TAD MORE DISCREET...
WHAT AREN'T YE TELLIN' ME? SCROOGEY WOULDN'T SAY A WORD. IT'S BEEN YEARS, BUT YE CAN TRUST ME... WHY ARE YOU TWO HIDIN'?
HMM! NOW THAT SCROOGE IS GONE, I GUESS HE WILLNAE MIND IF I TELL YE THE TRUTH...
A MONTH AGO, ONE MORNIN', HE CAME TO SEE ME AT THE THEATRE. SAID HE NEEDED ME TO DO SOME ACTIN'...

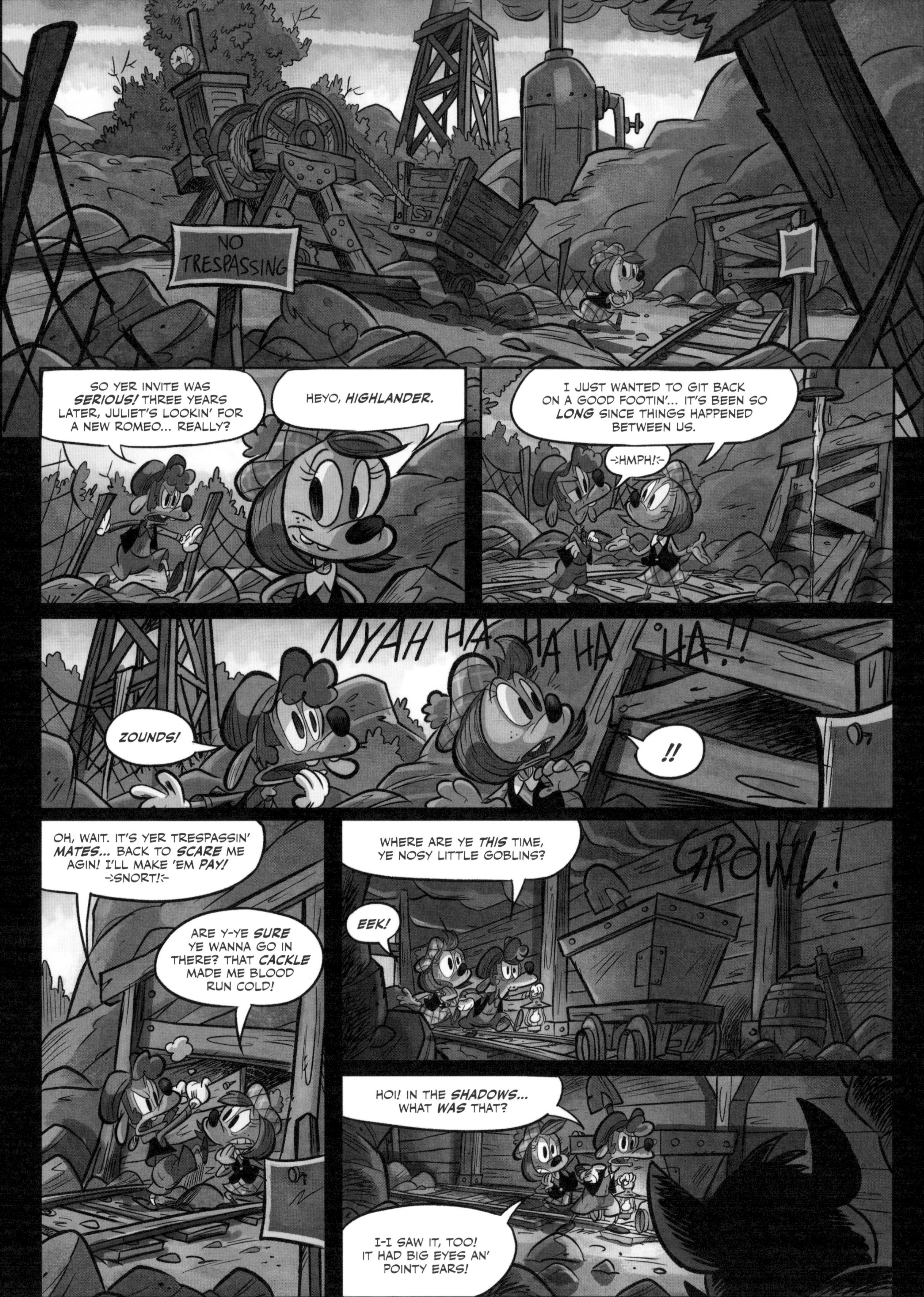
NO TRESPASSING
SO YER INVITE WAS SERIOUS! THREE YEARS LATER, JULIET'S LOOKIN' FOR A NEW ROMEO... REALLY?
HEYO, HIGHLANDER.
I JUST WANTED TO GIT BACK ON A GOOD FOOTIN'... IT'S BEEN SO LONG SINCE THINGS HAPPENED BETWEEN US.
-HMPH!-
NYAH HA HA HA HA!!
ZOUNDS!
!!
OH, WAIT. IT'S YER TRESPASSIN' MATES... BACK TO SCARE ME AGIN! I'LL MAKE 'EM PAY! -SNORT!-
ARE Y-YE SURE YE WANNA GO IN THERE? THAT CACKLE MADE ME BLOOD RUN COLD!
WHERE ARE YE THIS TIME, YE NOSY LITTLE GOBLINS?
GROWL!
EEK!
HOI! IN THE SHADOWS... WHAT WAS THAT?
I-I SAW IT, TOO! IT HAD BIG EYES AN' POINTY EARS!

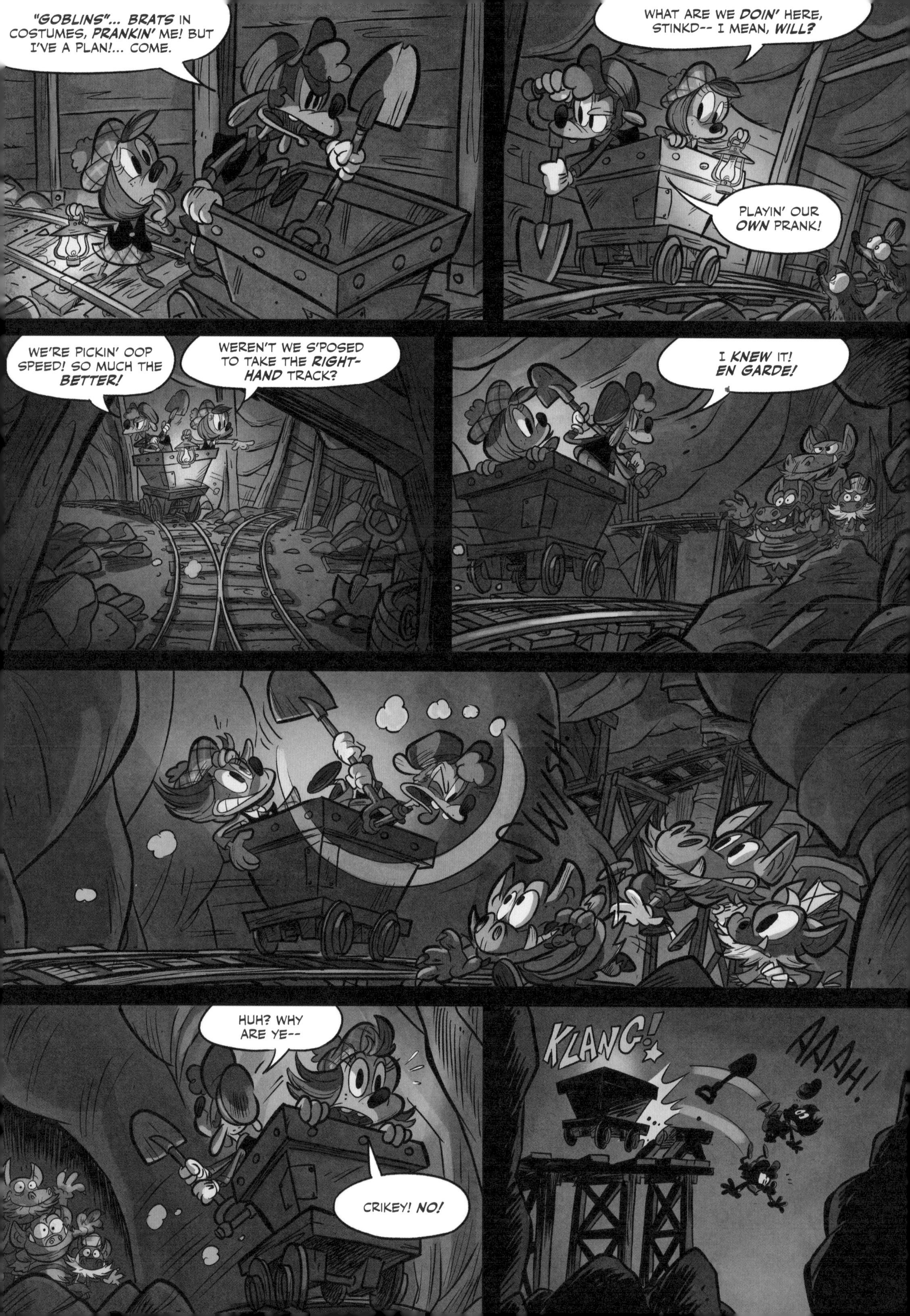
"GOBLINS"... BRATS IN COSTUMES, PRANKIN' ME! BUT I'VE A PLAN!... COME.
WHAT ARE WE DOIN' HERE, STINKD-- I MEAN, WILL?
PLAYIN' OUR OWN PRANK!
WE'RE PICKIN' OOP SPEED! SO MUCH THE BETTER!
WEREN'T WE S'POSED TO TAKE THE RIGHT-HAND TRACK?
I KNEW IT! EN GARDE!
HUH? WHY ARE YE--
CRIKEY! NO!
KLANG!
AAAH!

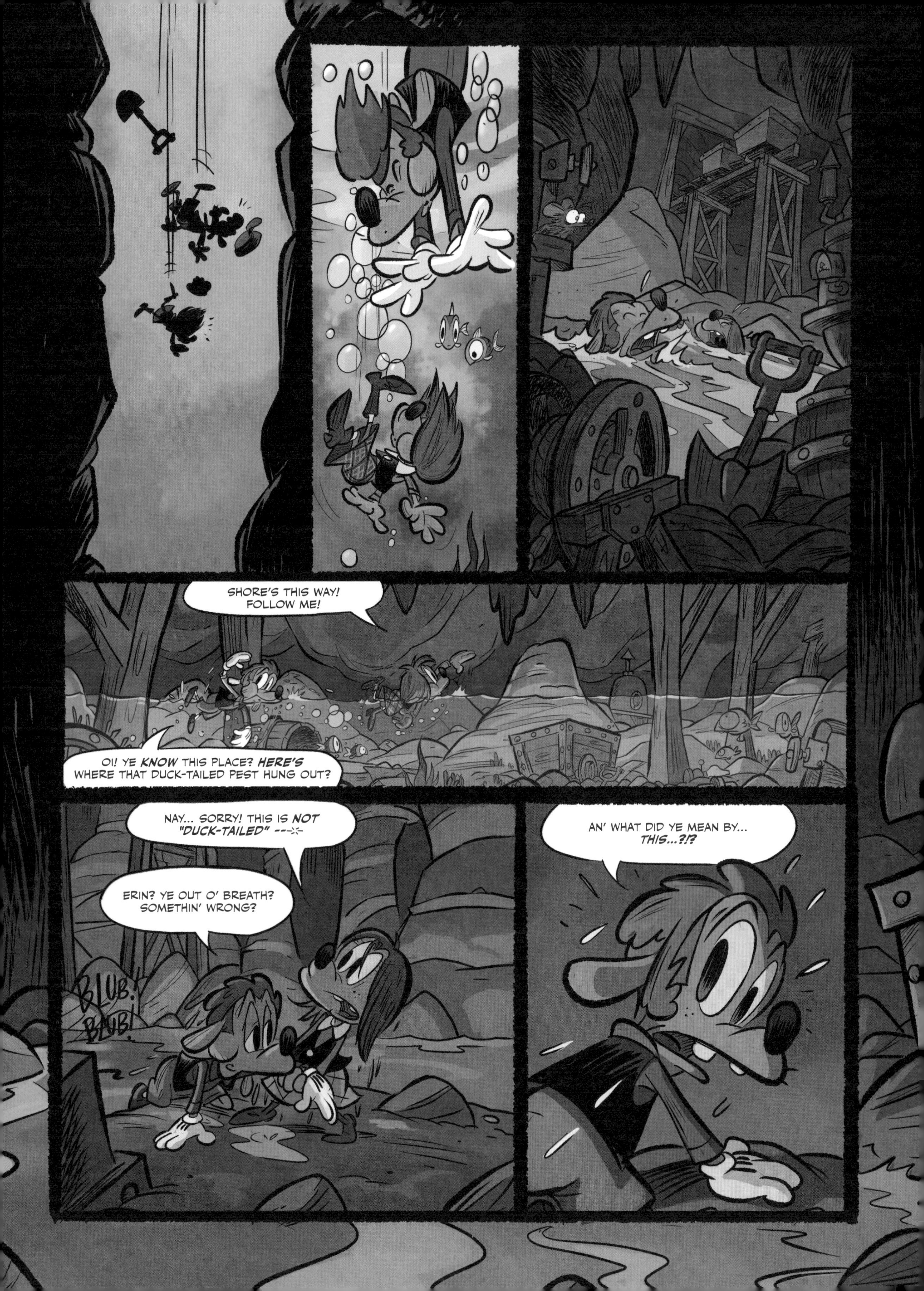
SHORE'S THIS WAY! FOLLOW ME!
OI! YE KNOW THIS PLACE? HERE'S WHERE THAT DUCK-TAILED PEST HUNG OUT?
NAY... SORRY! THIS IS NOT "DUCK-TAILED" ---
ERIN? YE OUT O' BREATH? SOMETHIN' WRONG?
BLUB! BLUB!
AN' WHAT DID YE MEAN BY... THIS...?!?

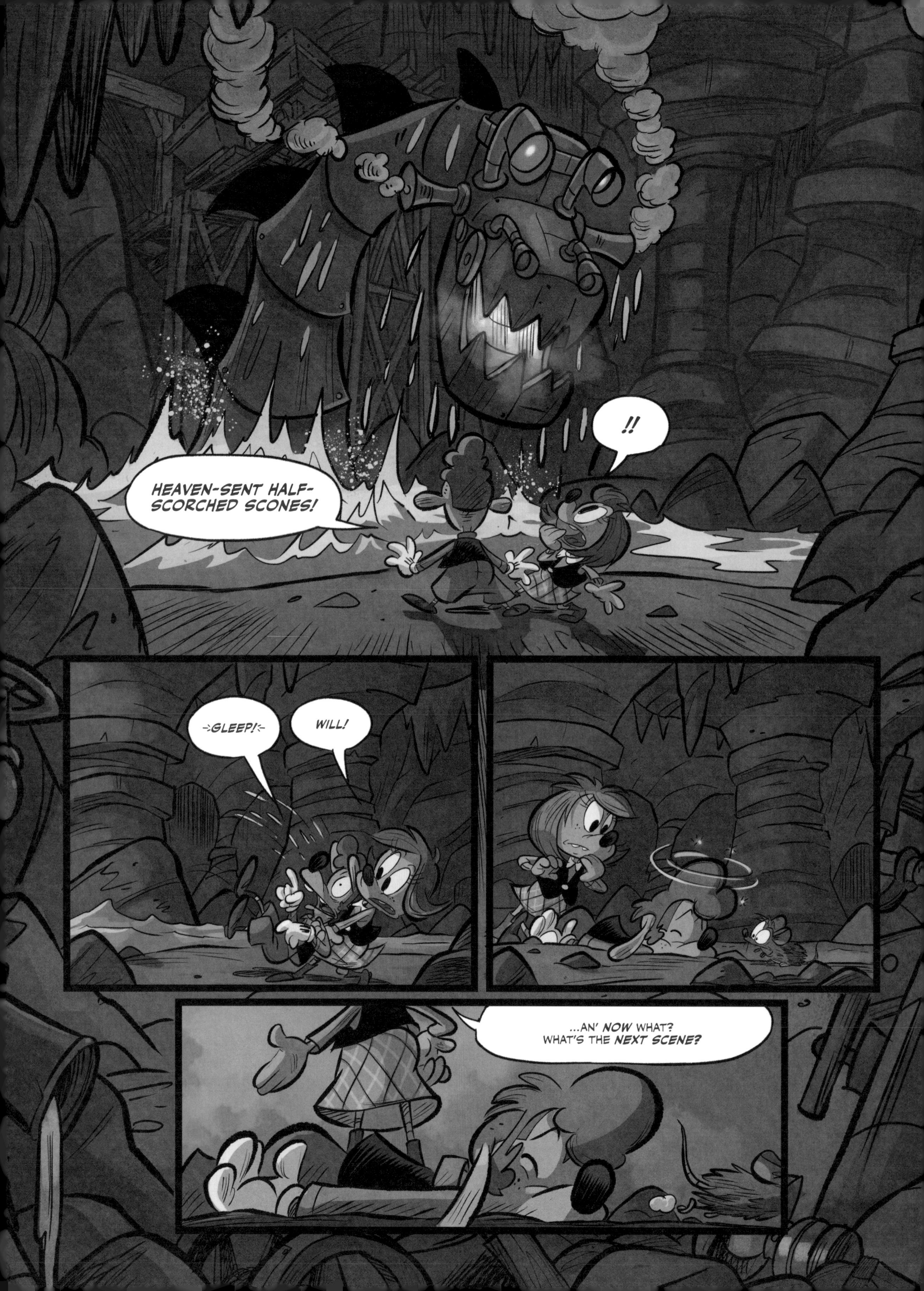
!!
HEAVEN-SENT HALF-SCORCHED SCONES!
-GLEEP!-
WILL!
...AN' NOW WHAT? WHAT'S THE NEXT SCENE?

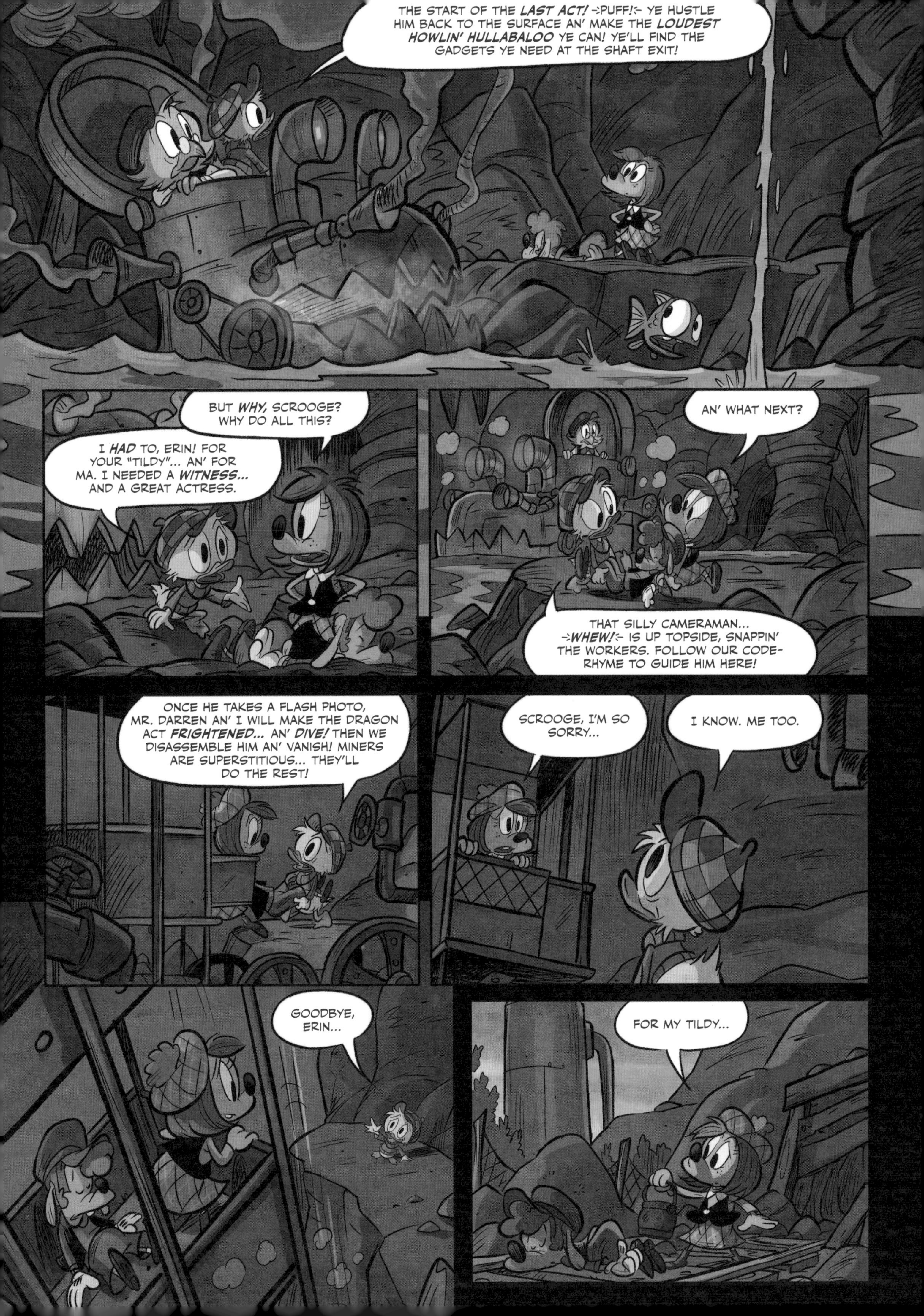
THE START OF THE LAST ACT! ->PUFF!<- YE HUSTLE HIM BACK TO THE SURFACE AN' MAKE THE LOUDEST HOWLIN' HULLABALOO YE CAN! YE'LL FIND THE GADGETS YE NEED AT THE SHAFT EXIT!
BUT WHY, SCROOGE? WHY DO ALL THIS?
I HAD TO, ERIN! FOR YOUR "TILDY"... AN' FOR MA. I NEEDED A WITNESS... AND A GREAT ACTRESS.
AN' WHAT NEXT?
THAT SILLY CAMERAMAN... ->WHEW!<- IS UP TOPSIDE, SNAPPIN' THE WORKERS. FOLLOW OUR CODE-RHYME TO GUIDE HIM HERE!
ONCE HE TAKES A FLASH PHOTO, MR. DARREN AN' I WILL MAKE THE DRAGON ACT FRIGHTENED... AN' DIVE! THEN WE DISASSEMBLE HIM AN' VANISH! MINERS ARE SUPERSTITIOUS... THEY'LL DO THE REST!
SCROOGE, I'M SO SORRY...
I KNOW. ME TOO.
GOODBYE, ERIN...
FOR MY TILDY...

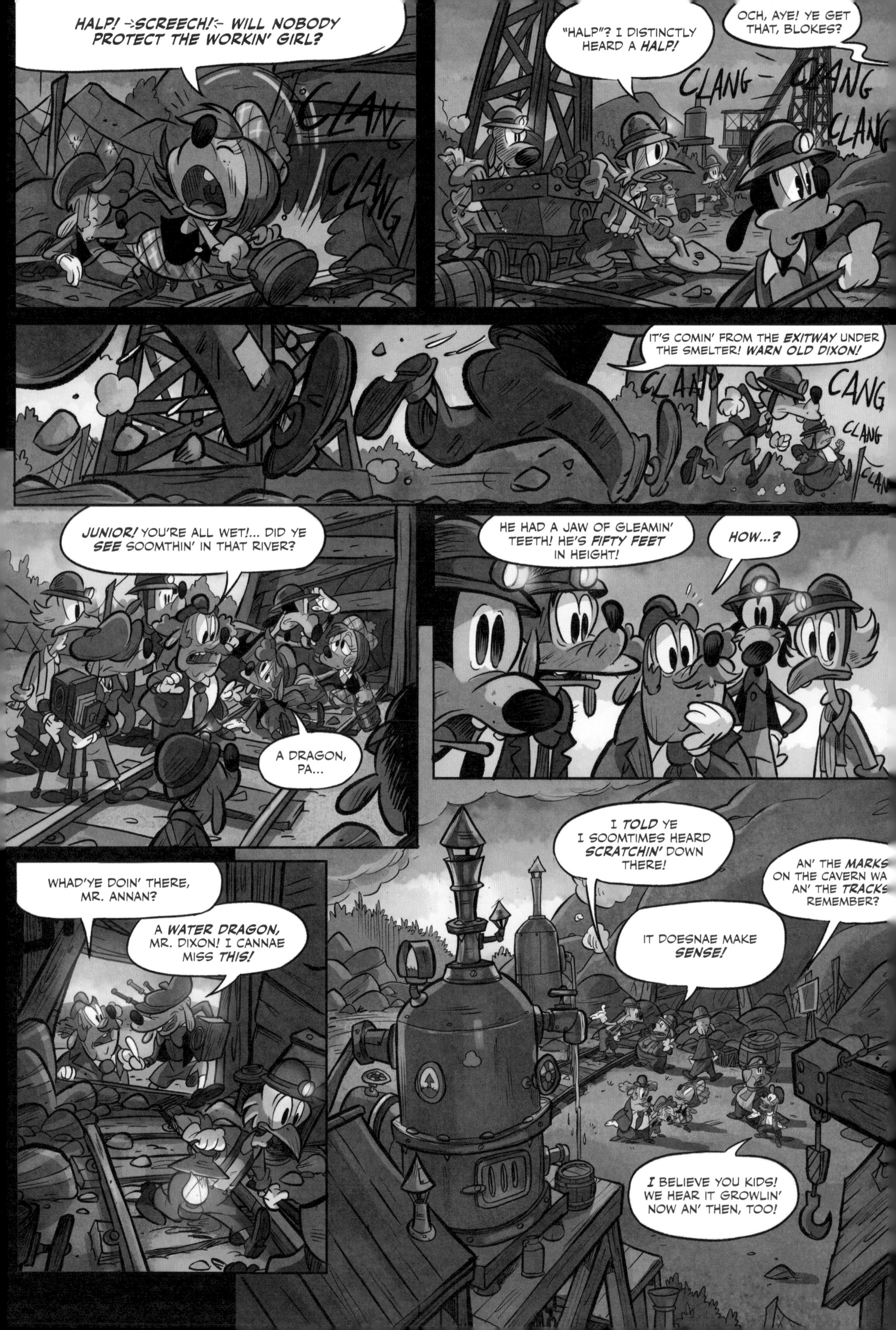
HALP! ->SCREECH!<- WILL NOBODY PROTECT THE WORKIN' GIRL?
CLANG
CLANG
"HALP"? I DISTINCTLY HEARD A HALP!
OCH, AYE! YE GET THAT, BLOKES?
CLANG
CLANG
CLANG
IT'S COMIN' FROM THE EXITWAY UNDER THE SMELTER! WARN OLD DIXON!
CLANG
CANG
CLANG
JUNIOR! YOU'RE ALL WET!... DID YE SEE SOOMTHIN' IN THAT RIVER?
A DRAGON, PA...
HE HAD A JAW OF GLEAMIN' TEETH! HE'S FIFTY FEET IN HEIGHT!
HOW...?
WHAD'YE DOIN' THERE, MR. ANNAN?
A WATER DRAGON, MR. DIXON! I CANNAE MISS THIS!
I TOLD YE I SOOMTIMES HEARD SCRATCHIN' DOWN THERE!
AN' THE MARKS ON THE CAVERN WA AN' THE TRACKS REMEMBER?
IT DOESNAE MAKE SENSE!
I BELIEVE YOU KIDS! WE HEAR IT GROWLIN' NOW AN' THEN, TOO!

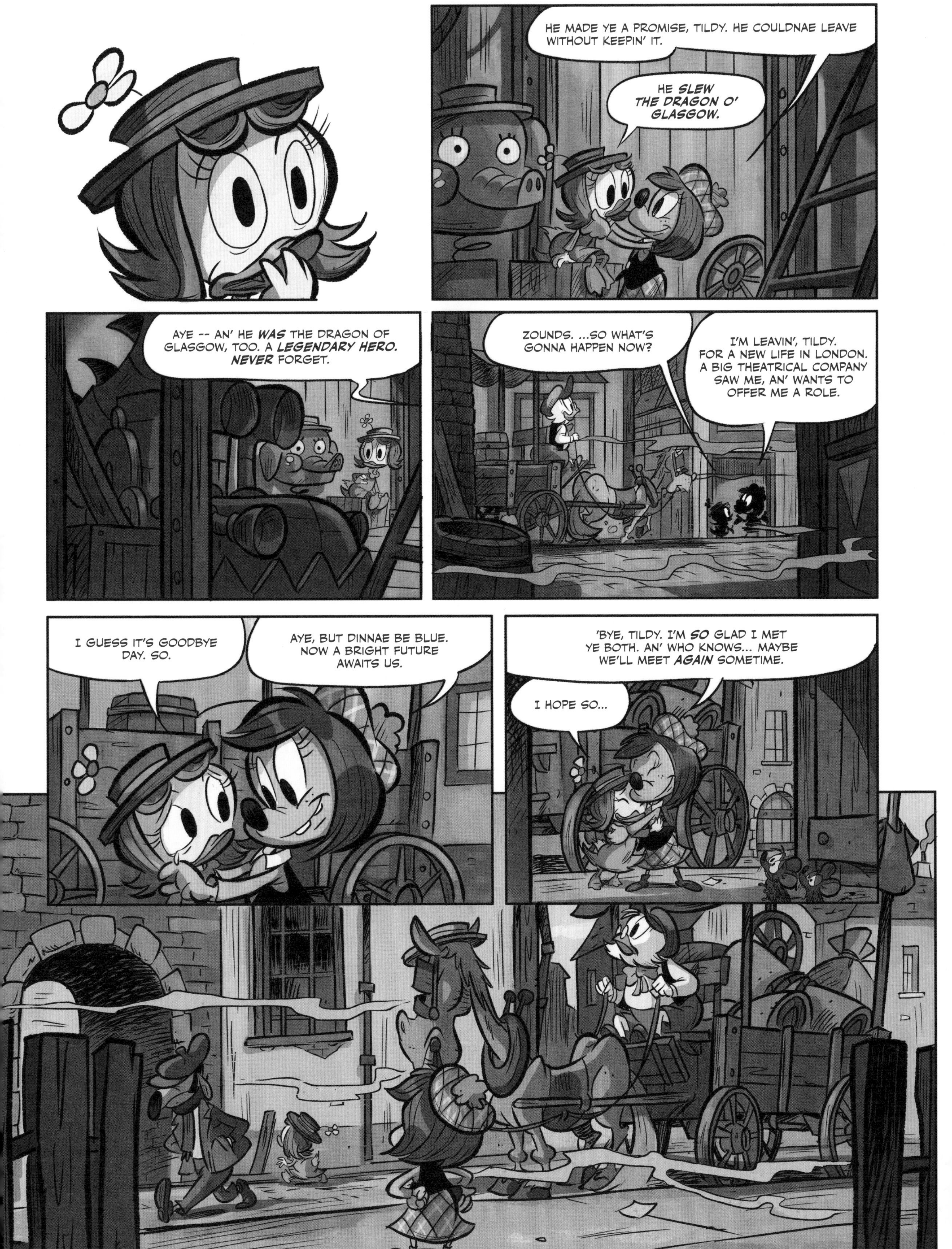
HE MADE YE A PROMISE, TILDY. HE COULDNAE LEAVE WITHOUT KEEPIN' IT.
HE SLEW THE DRAGON O' GLASGOW.
AYE -- AN' HE WAS THE DRAGON OF GLASGOW, TOO. A LEGENDARY HERO. NEVER FORGET.
ZOUNDS. ...SO WHAT'S GONNA HAPPEN NOW?
I'M LEAVIN', TILDY. FOR A NEW LIFE IN LONDON. A BIG THEATRICAL COMPANY SAW ME, AN' WANTS TO OFFER ME A ROLE.
I GUESS IT'S GOODBYE DAY. SO.
AYE, BUT DINNAE BE BLUE. NOW A BRIGHT FUTURE AWAITS US.
'BYE, TILDY. I'M SO GLAD I MET YE BOTH. AN' WHO KNOWS... MAYBE WE'LL MEET AGAIN SOMETIME.
I HOPE SO...

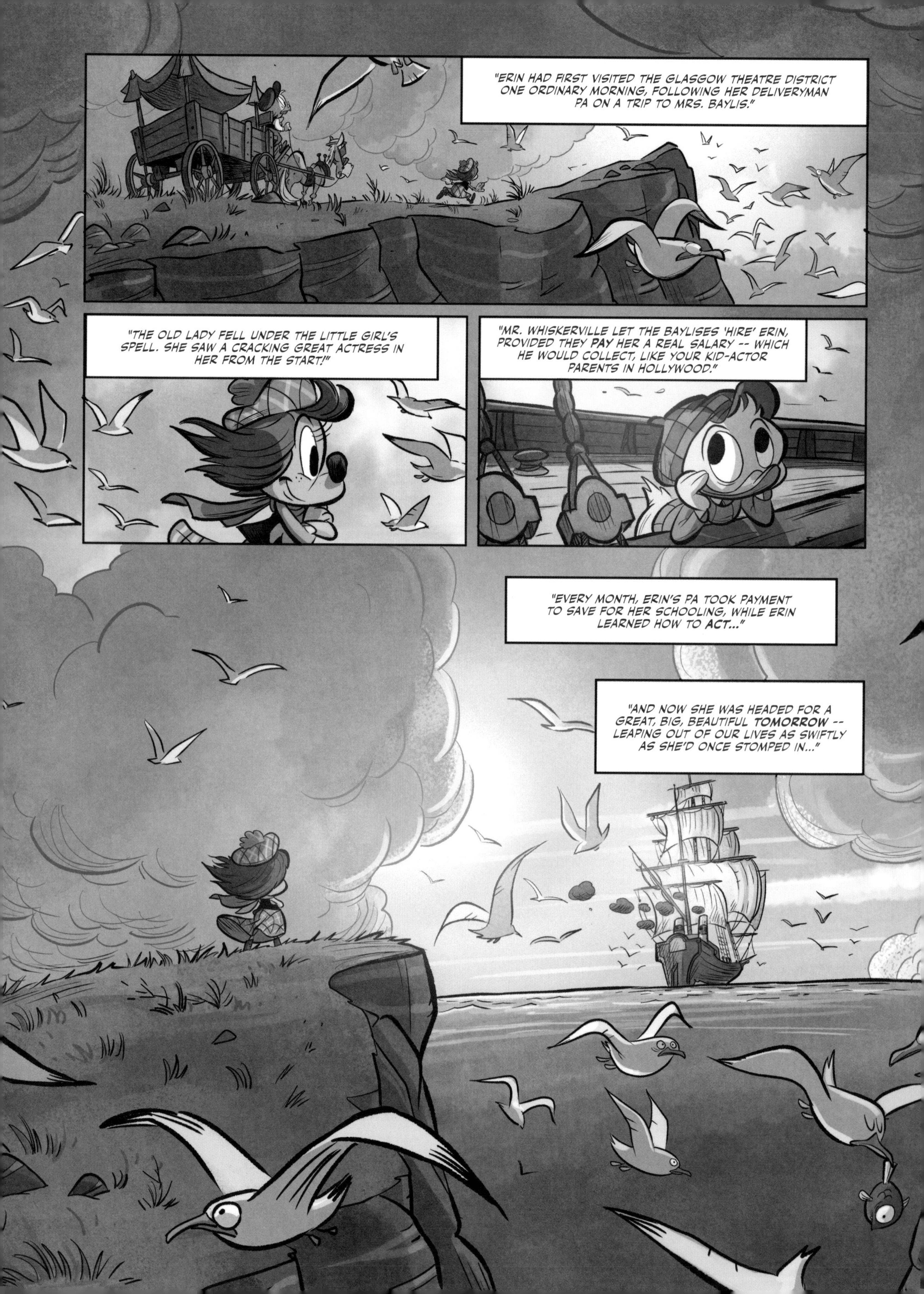
"ERIN HAD FIRST VISITED THE GLASGOW THEATRE DISTRICT ONE ORDINARY MORNING, FOLLOWING HER DELIVERYMAN PA ON A TRIP TO MRS. BAYLIS."
"THE OLD LADY FELL UNDER THE LITTLE GIRL'S SPELL. SHE SAW A CRACKING GREAT ACTRESS IN HER FROM THE START!"
"MR. WHISKERVILLE LET THE BAYLISES 'HIRE' ERIN, PROVIDED THEY PAY HER A REAL SALARY -- WHICH HE WOULD COLLECT, LIKE YOUR KID-ACTOR PARENTS IN HOLLYWOOD."
"EVERY MONTH, ERIN'S PA TOOK PAYMENT TO SAVE FOR HER SCHOOLING, WHILE ERIN LEARNED HOW TO ACT..."
"AND NOW SHE WAS HEADED FOR A GREAT, BIG, BEAUTIFUL TOMORROW -- LEAPING OUT OF OUR LIVES AS SWIFTLY AS SHE'D ONCE STOMPED IN..."

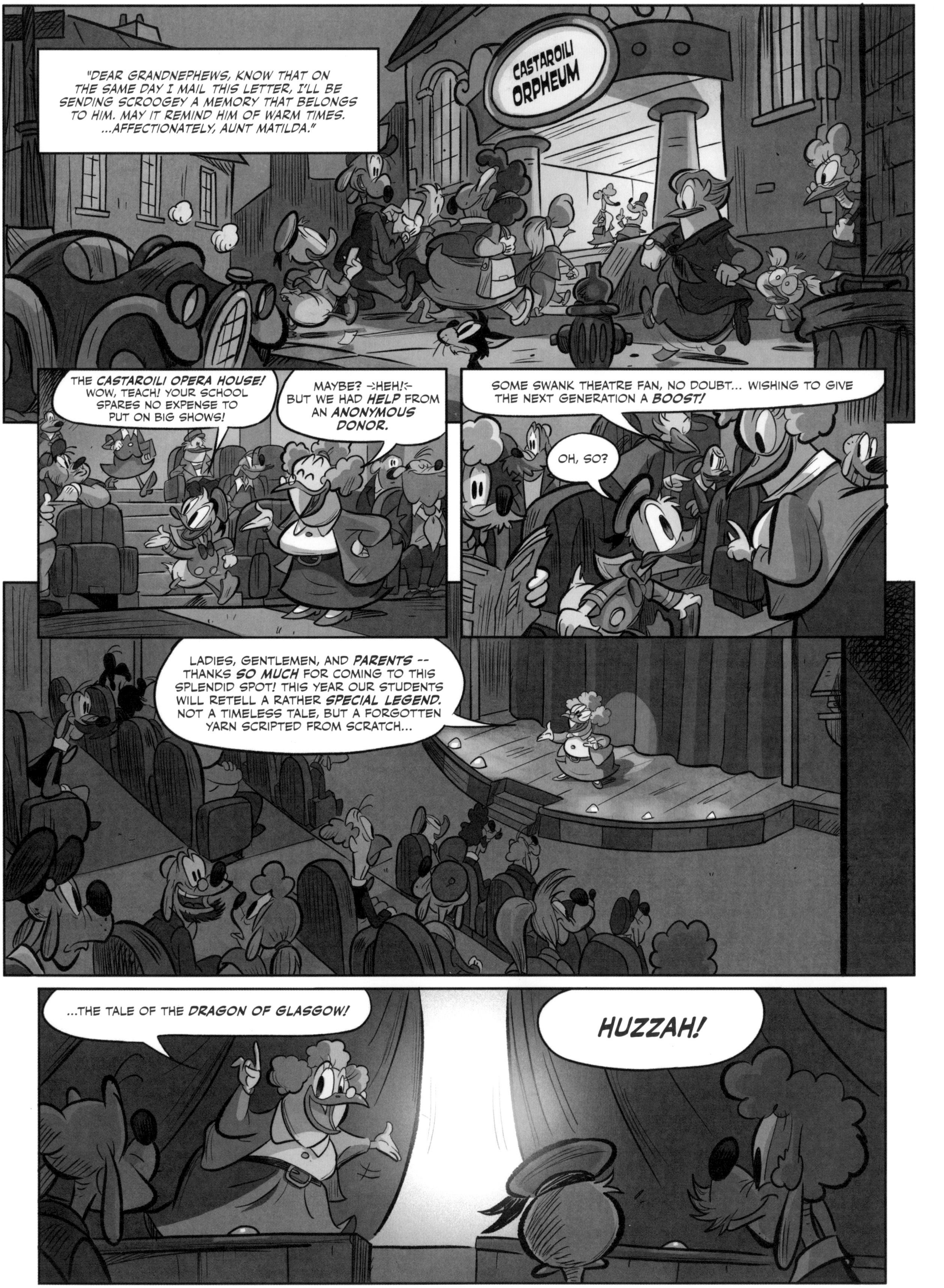

"DEAR GRANDNEPHEWS, KNOW THAT ON THE SAME DAY I MAIL THIS LETTER, I'LL BE SENDING SCROOGEY A MEMORY THAT BELONGS TO HIM. MAY IT REMIND HIM OF WARM TIMES. ...AFFECTIONATELY, AUNT MATILDA."
CASTAROILI ORPHEUM
THE CASTAROILI OPERA HOUSE! WOW, TEACH! YOUR SCHOOL SPARES NO EXPENSE TO PUT ON BIG SHOWS!
MAYBE? -HEH!- BUT WE HAD HELP FROM AN ANONYMOUS DONOR.
SOME SWANK THEATRE FAN, NO DOUBT... WISHING TO GIVE THE NEXT GENERATION A BOOST!
OH, SO?
LADIES, GENTLEMEN, AND PARENTS -- THANKS SO MUCH FOR COMING TO THIS SPLENDID SPOT! THIS YEAR OUR STUDENTS WILL RETELL A RATHER SPECIAL LEGEND. NOT A TIMELESS TALE, BUT A FORGOTTEN YARN SCRIPTED FROM SCRATCH...
...THE TALE OF THE DRAGON OF GLASGOW!
HUZZAH!

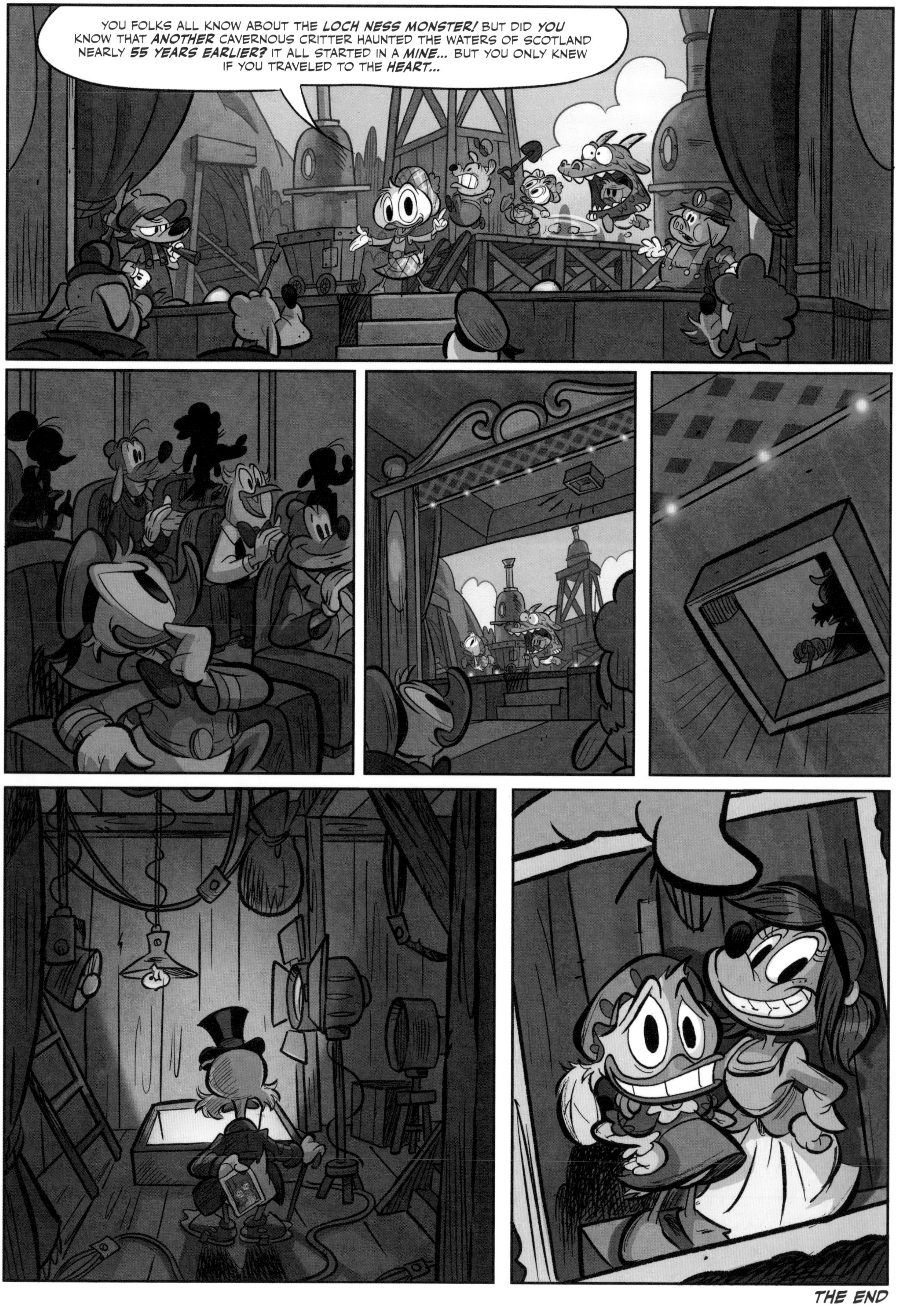
YOU FOLKS ALL KNOW ABOUT THE LOCH NESS MONSTER! BUT DID YOU KNOW THAT ANOTHER CAVERNOUS CRITTER HAUNTED THE WATERS OF SCOTLAND NEARLY 55 YEARS EARLIER? IT ALL STARTED IN A MINE... BUT YOU ONLY KNEW IF YOU TRAVELED TO THE HEART...
THE END

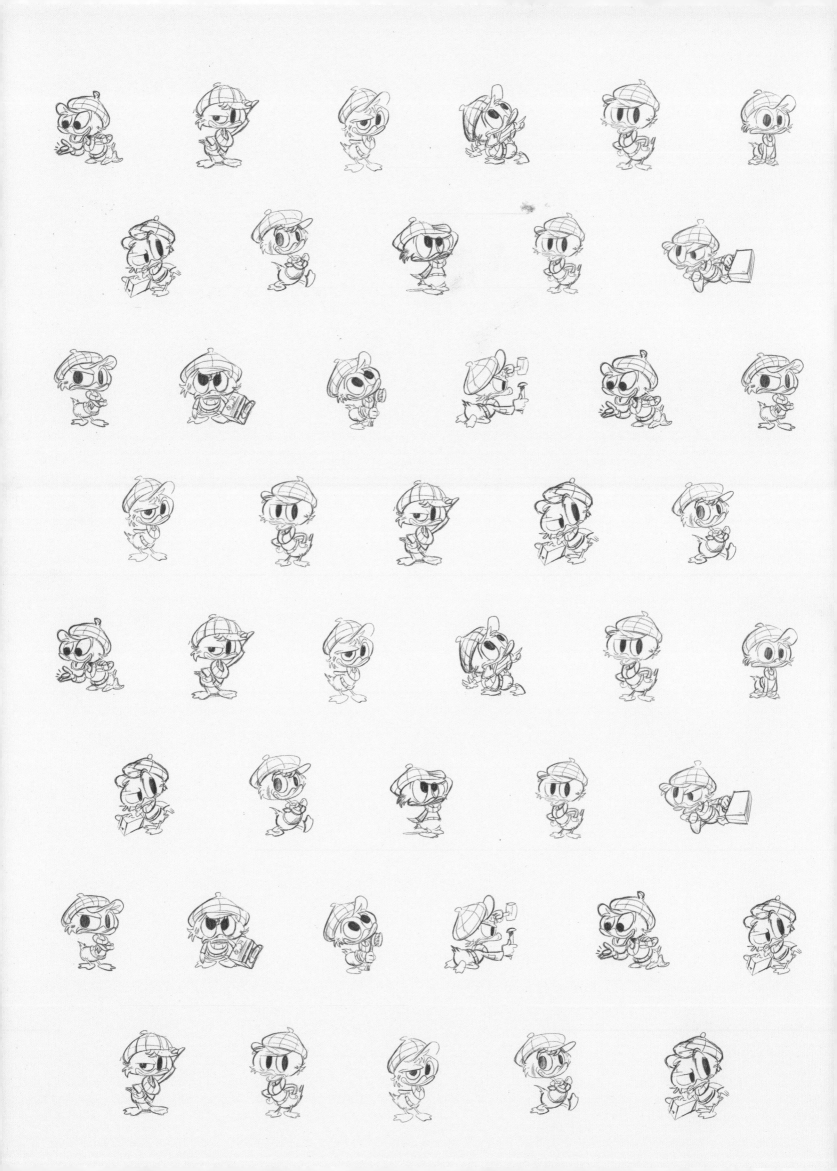